THE GOOD EARTH
BY
PEARL BUCK

Intelligent Education

INFLUENCE PUBLISHERS

Nashville, Tennessee

BRIGHT NOTES: The Good Earth

www.BrightNotes.com

No part of this publication may be used or reproduced in any manner whatsoever without written permission, except in the case of brief quotations in critical articles and reviews. For permissions, contact Influence Publishers http://www.influencepublishers.com.

ISBN: 978-1-645423-70-6 (Paperback)
ISBN: 978-1-645423-71-3 (eBook)

Published in accordance with the U.S. Copyright Office Orphan Works and Mass Digitization report of the register of copyrights, June 2015.

Originally published by Monarch Press.
Donald F. Roden; W. John Campbell, 1965
2019 Edition published by Influence Publishers.

Interior design by Lapiz Digital Services. Cover Design by Thinkpen Designs.

Printed in the United States of America.

Library of Congress Cataloging-in-Publication Data forthcoming.
Names: Intelligent Education
Title: BRIGHT NOTES: The Good Earth
Subject: STU004000 STUDY AIDS / Book Notes

CONTENTS

INTRODUCTION TO PEARL BUCK

BIRTH

On June 26, 1892, a daughter was born to Absalom and Caroline Sydenstricker. The child was named Pearl. The couple had been missionaries to China; but when Caroline became sick, they returned home to Hillsboro, West Virginia, where their daughter was born. In 1894, at the age of two, Pearl went to China with her parents. Her father was assigned to a mission at Chinkiang on the Yangtse River, and there Pearl spent the next six years of her life.

EARLY LIFE

These formative years spent in China were probably the most important ones in developing the ideas of Pearl Buck. She was not merely an American girl living in a white colony of some highly civilized Chinese city. Because her father was a missionary, her entire existence was rooted in that of the land in which she lived. She was a child living among the Chinese themselves. All her friends and her schoolmates were Chinese. Their language became familiar enough for her to think in. Moreover, her native land, America, was like a storybook place. Her parents told her about it, spoke its language, and preserved its customs in their dress and in the manner in which they lived within the privacy of their own home. Thus, the young Pearl became a sort of American Chinese. As she describes herself in her autobiography, *My Several Worlds*, she became "mentally bifocal." From her parents, she learned the American way of life. Her Chinese friends encouraged her to become one of them. In other words, in China she was like the European child, for example, that we all know in our own country. At home the parents preserve the Greek or Italian or Polish language and customs. On the streets and in school, the child learns the American way. Consequently, this young person's knowledge of people may be much broader than that of those of us who have been limited to the narrower confines of one culture and language.

BOXER REBELLION

It is difficult to fully appreciate how Pearl Buck felt in the year 1900 when her world began to crumble around her. From the time she was two years old, she had been loved and accepted by the Chinese people among whom she lived. In her autobiography she speaks, for example, of eating the Chinese food. This was something usually not done by foreigners who often were made violently ill by it. Yet she never got sick and seemed to develop the same kind of immunity that the Chinese themselves had. She had lived among these people not as a stranger, but as one of them. Therefore, when her Chinese friends stopped speaking to her and even began avoiding her, the child could not understand it. Her little world was shattered by something that happened hundreds of miles away.

A group of Chinese, referred to as Boxers, had convinced the Empress that all foreigners should be driven out of China. Chinese cities had been taken over by countries such as France and

England, who established colonies in them. European products were introduced to the medieval Chinese economy. At the same time, Europeans were buying raw materials from China at a cost much less than these could be gotten elsewhere. There was, of course, much advantage to China, since the Europeans also built railroads and introduced methods of sanitation unknown before. Some Chinese people, including the young Emperor Kwang-hsii, saw the advantages in the changes that the Europeans were making. However, an older, conservative group did not want things to change. Therefore, in 1990, a coup d'etat took place in which the young emperor was captured and imprisoned. Soon after this came the outbreaks against the foreigners. .

Pearl Buck's parents were Americans and missionaries. Neither of these groups had done anything to harm the Chinese. In fact, the missionaries, both European and American, had contributed much to Chinese health and education. Nevertheless, they were included in the group which the Boxers accused of introducing Western civilization into the old China world and were also to be driven out or killed. The Sydenstrickers did not leave willingly, however. Pearl's father took his family down to Shanghai only when he realized that it was absolutely necessary to do so.

EFFECT ON MISS BUCK

In her autobiography, Pearl Buck says that the full emotional effect of the Boxer Rebellion did not come to her until after her adventure was over. She had returned to America with her parents, and in September of 1901 was at her grandfather's farm in West Virginia. There she was told of the assassination of President McKinley. In her little girl's mind she connected this with the events in China. Her only thought was: "Must we have the revolution here, too?" With this she burst into tears.

This emotional outpouring resolved itself into a question which has perplexed Pearl Buck all of her adult life. The Christian culture of the West teaches that love and brotherhood must be the rule of life. By the same token, Asian culture teaches that life is sacred, and that it is evil to kill even a beast. Yet these two groups cannot get along with each other, or even sometimes with themselves. Why then this dichotomy between the thought and the deed, between the philosophies and the lives of men?

LATER LIFE

Pearl's early education had been given her by tutors and at the mission school in Chinkiang. At fifteen she was sent to boarding school in Shanghai. Afterwards, at seventeen, she was enrolled at Randolph-Macon College in Virginia. She graduated in 1914, and then taught psychology there for one semester. On May 13, 1917, she married Dr. John Lossing Buck. Although they were divorced in 1935, the author had always used the name Pearl S. Buck professionally.

Between the years 1917 to 1925, Miss Buck taught English at the University of Nanking, at Southeastern University and at Chung Yang University. Since she had spoken both Chinese and English from her early childhood, she was well qualified for this work. In 1925, however, she went to Cornell University with her husband. Here she received her Master of Arts degree in English.

PUBLICATIONS

Although Pearl Buck had previously published articles in various magazines, her first novel *East Wind: West Wind* did not appear until 1930. This work, however, did not attract much attention.

In 1931, the author published the novel upon which her entire reputation as a writer very probably rests. *The Good Earth* was published as the first novel in a proposed trilogy. *Sons* appeared in 1932, and *A House Divided* came out in 1935. In this year also, *House of Earth*, a collected edition of these three novels, was published.

OTHER WORKS

A list of Pearl Buck's other novels, classified according to theme, can be found in the Bibliography section of this study guide. Here it is appropriate to mention the two biographies which she wrote about her parents: *The Exile* and *Fighting Angel*, both published in 1936. The first of these, *The Exile*, had actually been written years before, but had never been published. These works, perhaps even more than any of her novels including. *The Good Earth*, show the author's intense interest in people. In them she tells the story of her parents and of their struggle for the people of China. Their intention was not simply to bring to these people religion as dogma, but to bring to them the strength and love of Christianity.

THE GOOD EARTH

Published in 1931, *The Good Earth* is probably the author's best work. In it she attempts to describe the cycle of life: beginning the story with her hero as a young man and completing it with his death. This novel aroused mixed reactions among both Americans and Chinese. Many Americans who regarded the story as too Chinese had difficulty identifying with it. On the other hand, many Chinese did not think it oriental enough. They regarded its subject - the peasant farmer - as unworthy of a book about China. These aristocratic Chinese intellectuals wanted the world to see their country as a center of culture and good living. But history has proven them wrong. Centuries of corrupt rule finally caused the country to collapse under the weight of its own inequities. The long-suffering farmer - the backbone of this agricultural land - was virtually given over to the most ruthless of his oppressors, the Communists.

Some comment on this subject was printed in the January 15, 1933, edition of the *New York Times*. Professor Kiang KangHu wrote a letter containing the following criticisms of Pearl Buck's work:

"Her portrait of China may be quite faithful from her point of view ... she seems to enjoy more depicting certain peculiarities and defects than presenting ordinary human figures ... Pearl Buck is more of a caricature cartoonist than a portrait painter ... Very often I felt uneasy at her minute descriptions of certain peculiarities and defects of some lowly bred Chinese characters ... she portrays her own young life in China as much under the influence of Chinese coolies and amahs ... They may form the majority of the Chinese population, but they are certainly not characteristic of the Chinese people."

What the professor objected to, therefore, was the author's selectivity: her focus on the hardships of the peasant farmer, borne with stoic courage, instead of the cultural lives of the upper class, certainly atypical of the China she knew. Pearl Buck answered these objections in a letter printed in the Times on the same day as the professor's. Perhaps the most important part of it is her concluding remarks:

"As to whether I am doing China a service or not in my books only time can tell. I have received many

letters from people who tell me they have become interested in China ... I can write only what I know and I know nothing but China, having always lived there ... I write about the people I do know ... the people in China I love best to live among, the everyday people ..."

Time has proven Pearl Buck right. The Chinese intellectuals with little concern for the realities of life failed to make China a strong, united nation. In their place, the Communists have been able to cash in on their policies and drive the last vestige of hope from the land.

SUCCESS

Although *The Good Earth* is a controversial novel, it has enjoyed considerable success. It was a best seller and won the Pulitzer Prize for its author. Since its appearance, it has been translated into more than thirty languages. In 1932, Owen and Donald Davis dramatized it; later the story was made into a very successful movie. The reason for the success of *The Good Earth* is simple. It tells of a man's struggle for life, for success, and for happiness. The concretes of this struggle may be of a Chinese farmer acting in his particular context, but the abstract meaning of his struggle - for existence and happiness - has a universality not limited by the geographic boundaries of China.

NOBEL PRIZE

When Pearl Buck was declared the winner in 1938 of the Nobel Prize for literature, a storm of protest went up. Many people thought that she had not contributed enough to world literature to deserve such a great prize. But perhaps these people were looking only at the concretes of her fiction. The abstractions involved in her stories had universal appeal and she had written with understanding of human beings weathering severe hardships. In addition, she had written two biographies in which she showed a man and a woman struggling to succeed in their chosen professions - as missionaries. After all, the purpose of the Nobel Prize is to reward those who are trying to promote peace and understanding among mankind. This is what Pearl Buck is trying to do. Anders Osterling in *Nobel: The Man and His Prizes* summed up the selection of Miss Buck in these words:

> **"The decisive factor in the Academy's judgment was, above all, the admirable biographies of her parents ... two volumes which seemed to deserved classic rank and to possess the required prospects for permanent interest."**

OTHER HONORS

The list of awards and honors which Pearl Buck has received during her lifetime is too long to include here. She has received honorary degrees from universities like Yale. She is a member of the American Academy of Arts and Sciences. Her books have received many individual awards.

PEARL BUCK, THE PERSON

When reading the works of Pearl Buck, one very quickly discovers that the author's sympathies lie greatly with the Chinese. Yet it is not a political or a religious interest. Her interest is in people for themselves; and, as she has so often said, the Chinese are the people she knows best. In 1900, and again in 1927, she had had to flee because she was not Chinese. At present she is living in America and will probably never see China again because of the Communist takeover. However, Miss Buck continues to work to help her people. In 1949, for example, she founded Welcome House where American born orphans of Asian ancestry could live until new homes were found for them. In this way she continues the work which her parents did before her, and which she herself did for so many years as a missionary and teacher in China.

THE GOOD EARTH

CHAPTER ONE

The story begins on the wedding day of Wang Lung. He rises early, bathes himself, and goes into town where he is to meet his bride. Because his mother is dead, he must shop for the food for the wedding feast; at the market he buys some pork and some beef. He has himself shaven at the barber's so as to present a perfectly clean appearance when he meets his bride. When he first goes to the House of Hwang for O-lan, his bride, he is frightened; he leaves and returns later. The gateman brings Wang Lung in to the Old Mistress who gives O-lan to him and the two return together to the house of Wang Lung's father. On the way, the young man stops to burn incense before the gods. That evening some friends and relatives come to the house to help Wang Lung celebrate his wedding. O-lan prepares the food, but she does not appear before the strange men since she cannot be seen by others until after the first night of marriage.

COMMENT

In this chapter the author paints a picture quite different from the conventional American wedding. There was no big church ceremony; neither was there any great feasting with the families of the bride and groom helping the two young people to celebrate. The reader might get the impression that marriage was not important to the Chinese, yet, if he observes closely, he sees that this is not so. Wang Lung's father gone earlier to the House of Hwang with jewelry for the bride. Wang Lung himself was extremely happy on his wedding day and made great personal preparation for it. The ceremony, such as it was, was performed by the Old Mistress who gave O-lan to her husband. Note the instructions that she gave the young girl about obeying and serving her new husband. Observe also that the Old Mistress told Wang Lung the story of O-lan's life as she knew it. Finally, the burning of incense before the gods was to invoke a blessing on the marriage.

The wedding feast itself was a strange affair. O-lan prepared the food, but she did not appear at the feast. This is in keeping with the old oriental idea of the role of the woman. Her job is primarily to be a servant to her husband and a mother to his children. She does not share his life in the way that American women do. However, this does not mean that there is no love. Wang Lung was conscious enough of his bride as a person to want a pretty wife and not one that was ugly or that had pockmarks. Observe also that he bought her some peaches to eat, and that he was happy when she touched the incense to signify their union.

The **theme** of the novel is also introduced in this chapter. Note that Wang Lung is a farmer. One of the first things he does when he arises is to notice the weather. He is happy that there is rain coming in a day or two. Notice too the repeated use of the word earth: "the earth would bear fruit"; "there was a thick wall of earth"; "the gods were earth gods." Thus does the author emphasize what she is going to write about in this novel. It is the story of a man's struggle to eke out an existence from the land.

In this chapter also, the author subtly introduces us to the changes that are about to take place in China. Notice that Wang Lung wears his hair in the braid which is characteristic of the men of the old China. At the stall of the barber, he was told that the new style is to cut off the braid. But Wang Lung cannot do this without first asking his father. Thus for the time being, he stayed with the old ways.

Lastly, the author introduces us to the main characters in the story. There is Wang Lung, his father, and O-lan, and there is the uncle and his family. All of these people will play important parts in the novel. Nor is the House of Hwang with its many courts to be forgotten: it too will achieve a place of importance in the story.

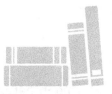

THE GOOD EARTH

CHAPTER TWO

....

We learn next of the first days of the marriage. On the first morning O-lan arises and prepares hot water for the old father.

Then she brings her husband tea. Wang Lung had to perform these tasks before his marriage, but now his wife will do them for him. He can tend to the fields and then come home to find his meals prepared for him. O-lan silently takes upon herself the household duties. First she cleans the entire house which had been cared for by the two men during the six years since Wang Lung's mother had died. Then she goes out to gather fuel to spare the men the task. She also goes out to the crossroads to gather manure that could be used for fertilizer. Nothing seems to escape her, and she never has to be told anything. One day, after her household chores are completed, she takes a hoe and goes out into the fields, where she works for the rest of the day beside her husband.

COMMENT

Here we get an image of a poor, hardworking and earnestly beautiful young couple. Their beauty is projected by their sense of inner worth and by the development of the relationship.

O-lan knew what her responsibility was, and she went about her work willingly and silently. Before her marriage she had been a slave and had worked for nothing but her master's pleasure. Now she was a partner working with her husband to help bring success to their venture.

Wang Lung is a proud young husband, pleased with his wife. Although he knew that she had to come with him, he wanted her to be pleased with him. His oriental philosophy told him that it is the woman's place only to serve. Yet he is also a man, and the nature of man is to want his mate to desire him. Therefore, he spent his time thinking of O-lan and hoping that she like him for himself. When she brought him tea in his hot water, he was greatly pleased.

The **theme** of the story is reflected by Wang Lung working in the fields, and feeling that his labors were joyous because he was sharing his life with someone he valued. Occasionally he turned a piece of brick or a piece of old wood out of the ground and reflected that those were signs that other people, now dead, once lived upon that same spot. He considered that someday he too would be gone, but this was his turn on the earth. This was his time to make things grow out of it. He thought of land as the only permanent thing, which would last until the end of time. The **theme** is re-emphasized at the end of the chapter when O-lan announced to her husband that she was going to have a child. In this way, just as new life continues to come out of the earth, new life will come out of the union of these two people. The world will continue to move on with this new life which is being created.

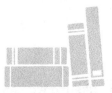

THE GOOD EARTH

CHAPTER THREE

This section tells the story of the birth of the first child. As the time grows near, Wang Lung tells his wife that they should have a woman in to help her, but O-lan will not hear of this. When Wang Lung mentions the House of Hwang, she becomes angry. She will not go to the house again until she can bring her son, dressed in a red coat and red-flowered trousers. On his head she will place a hat with a gilded Buddha and on his feet tiger-faced shoes. Wang Lung is amazed at his wife's plans, but he gives her the money for the cloth. When the time comes, she goes into the bedroom by herself; a few hours later, she delivers her own child, a son. Wang Lung is proud of what has happened: his wife has proven herself a strong woman, and he now has a son. He buys eggs, according to the custom, and dyes them red. These are distributed in the village as a sign of what has happened.

COMMENT

O-lan had never been a talkative woman. However, when Wang Lung mentioned the House of Hwang, she became disturbed and told her husband her plan for visiting the House of Hwang with the baby. In this scene the setting may be Chinese, but the character personifies woman. O-lan had thought about her child and planned for it before it was even born. She pictured it dressed in the fancy clothes that she would make for it, and envisioned a great satisfaction when she returned to the Great House where she was once a kitchen slave, carrying her infant and mistress of her own being.

When Wang Lung gives his wife money for the baby's garments, the earth-theme comes sharply into focus. He explained the value of his silver: he worked his land and sold the product for money. He felt, then, that the silver was part of him - his energy had gone into the earth and the silver came out of it. He gave the money to O-lan willingly, to express the great love he felt for her and their child.

Because of touches like the poor hut and the un-attended mother this scene might arouse a sense of pity. However, it is in reality a scene of joy: Wang Lung is the proud father who could not even eat until his son was born. He was touched by the sight of his wife lying in the bed so peacefully, and tremendously proud of her and the child. He tried to reward her with the special treat of the red sugar stirred into boiling water, and bought his eggs to distribute so that the whole village could share in his joy.

THE GOOD EARTH

CHAPTER FOUR

. . . .

The day after the child was born, O-lan arose prepared food for the men. After the noon hour, Wang Lung got dressed and went into town to buy his sugar and eggs. O-lan did not work in the field with her husband for a time. However, after she had regained her strength, she was out there once more with him. The child would lie on a quilt placed on the ground. When he was hungry, he would cry, and then O-lan fed him. After the harvests were gathered, and the winter crops planted, there was great abundance in the house of Wang Lung, but he and his wife were not wasteful. They would not throw away anything that could be repaired, nor would they buy anything that they could make themselves. Thus when the product was sold from the year's abundant crop, Wang Lung had some extra silver dollars left over. O-lan dug a hole in the bedroom wall, and the silver was stored in it. This gave her husband a feeling of great security.

COMMENT

The beginning of this chapter re-emphasizes the joy of the young father by relating the incident at the grocer's. The words of the older man make Wang Lung very proud, but they also make him fearful. He is having so much good fortune that he thinks something dreadful might happen. Therefore, he lights four sticks of incense to the gods in the little temple. The remainder of the chapter provides a contrast. Wang Lung is a hard worker and a very thrifty man. His wife is also very thrifty and does not waste anything. He is shrewd enough to save his grain until later in the season when the prices are higher. Therefore, his house is filled with abundance, and he even has extra silver. On the other hand, other farmers are not like this. His uncle, for example, is very extravagant: he is not careful about either his crops or his money and consequently has nothing. Here the author presents the reader with the two extremes of man - the hard worker and the lazy one. She does not ask us to make a choice because hers is obviously Wang Lung and O-lan.

There are two other points to be noted in this chapter. First, the author very clearly demonstrates the favored treatment that the rich receive. When Wang Lung was in the store alone, the grocer paid him all sorts of compliments and spent time with him. As soon as a well-dressed man came in, the grocer immediately left Wang Lung and went to the newcomer. Secondly, Miss Buck presents some Chinese customs. For example, the winter time is a time of visiting and hospitality. Note, however, that Wang Lung did not do much of this. He was afraid that others might see his abundance and become jealous of him. This, one might imagine, would be a typical reaction of a Chinese farmer; a poor man who suddenly finds himself with a certain wealth. He hides it so that he will not have to share it with anyone.

THE GOOD EARTH

CHAPTER FIVE

. . . .

The celebration of the New Year and the visit to the House of Hwang are the next parts of the story. Wang Lung went into town and bought some articles which were needed for the celebration. On each part of the house and on every tool and utensil, litter signs with symbols of riches and of luck were pasted. Then Wang Lung burned a little incense in front of the earth gods. O-lan took some pork fat and some rice flour, and from these she made cookies like those which she had made at the Great House. These were not to be given to their own guests, but were to be carried as a gift to the Old Mistress. On the second day of the New Year, dressed in their new clothes, the couple went to the House of Hwang. There O-lan presented her child for the Old Mistress to see. On the way home, she told her husband that she thought the family in the Great House was not prospering. Hearing that a piece of property that belonged to the House of Hwang was for sale, Wang Lung determined to buy it.

COMMENT

Here we see the results of the hard work of Wang Lung and O-lan: they are able to afford expensive cakes and clothes. This is contrasted with the squalor of the House of Hwang where not even the Old Mistress has a new coat. There they have squandered their money and have reached the point where they must sell some of their land. Wang Lung wants to buy it for two reasons: first he realizes the value of land - it is a person's flesh and blood; secondly, it is a point of pride with him and with O-lan. The woman had been a slave in that house, but now her husband will own some of its land.

The reader should note the superstition of the Chinese couple. They are cautious not to let their relatives and neighbors see their wealth. Then, when they find themselves talking about their good fortune while they are out on the road, they try to turn away the evil spirits by lies. Wang Lung says loudly that he is cursed with a girl who is covered with pockmarks. Then he hides his son's head under his own coat so that nobody will see him. In this manner, he tries to protect his family.

A little incident shows a change that is coming over Wang Lung. In the house of the gatekeeper, he acts in a proud manner. When he is given tea, he ignores it and does not drink it; this is to give the impression that it is not good enough for him. Just a year before this, he had been afraid even to approach the Great House. Now, however, he acts as though he is a man of great wealth who is lowering himself to come there.

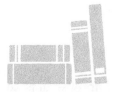

THE GOOD EARTH

When Wang Lung went to buy the land, the Old Lord was still sleeping although it was past noon. Therefore, the young man had to deal with the Old Lord's agent. This was not pleasant for the agent did not have the interest in the transaction that Wang Lung had. Once the land was purchased, the young farmer did not know whether or not he had done the right thing. But that summer he worked hard, and O-lan worked alongside him even though she was again pregnant. However, when her time came she delivered her own child once more, and returned immediately to the field. Wang Lung was happy at the birth of a second son. That year was another good one for him: the crops were abundant, and he had more silver to store in his hole in the earthen wall. What made him especially happy, however, was the fact that rice from the land of Hwang brought twice the price of his other rice. Now everyone was proud of him, and they spoke of making him the head of the village.

COMMENT

The emphasis in this chapter seems to shift to the person of O-lan. Throughout the first chapters, we see her hard work and her thrift; here the author shows her as a tremendously strong woman. Although pregnant, she works side by side with her husband. Even after giving birth to her child, she returns to the field to work. Wang Lung exclaims that this woman has brought nothing but good fortune to his house.

The endurance of O-lan might seem difficult to believe. However, it is a thing which does exist. In our country we are used to seeing the modern woman who must have all kinds of special care. But even in America, during the pioneer days, women were known to deliver their own children, and then to return to the fields. In their necessity, they were strong enough to do these things.

In this chapter Wang Lung is faced with a choice. Which is better to have, silver or land? He chose land even though it was just a small piece. Two hundred paces by one hundred and twenty paces is only about the size of two football fields. However, because it was good, fertile land, Wang Lung was able to get a good crop from it. Thus, he had more silver to replace what he had spent on the plot. More importantly, he had a good piece of ground that he could farm every year.

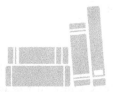

THE GOOD EARTH

CHAPTER SEVEN

Wang Lung is very much disturbed because the family of his uncle are a worthless lot. When he met his eldest girl cousin in the village talking to some men, he went to his uncle's wife to complain. The next day his uncle came to the field where he was working. The two men began in the polite Chinese style. However, Wang Lung became angry at his uncle and spoke harshly to him. At this, the uncle slapped him because it is a fault for a young man to correct an elder. The uncle then threatened to tell the whole village what his nephew had done, and Wang Lung was forced to lend him money. He went into the house to get it. There he found that O-lan given birth to her third child that day - it was girl. Going back out to the field, Wang Lung was very angry because he knew that his uncle would never pay him back. Nevertheless, Wang Lung had had no choice but to "lend" the money to his father's brother. This was Chinese custom.

COMMENT

Miss Buck here introduces some of the less pleasant aspects of Chinese life. Wang Lung is bound by a strict code which is based upon honor and the paying of homage to one's elders; he must follow this code no matter how difficult it might be, or else he will be disgraced. Therefore, although his uncle's family is a lazy group, Wang Lung must help them. The uncle, who is not too concerned about his honor, allows his daughter to go through the village and talk openly with men. He uses Wang Lung's virtues - his sense of honor - to extract money from him. He knows that Wang Lung does not want to be disgraced in public.

Another premise presented here is the Chinese attitude towards women. O-lan had worked side by side with her husband in the fields; she had done everything within her power to help him. Nevertheless, when she gives birth to a girl baby, it is a time of sadness, an evil omen. Even O-lan says, "It is only a slave this time." The girl baby in Chinese life was not considered a blessing, since the family had to support her until she could be married. She could never fully earn her keep because by the time she was old enough to work in the fields, she was usually married.

Wang Lung's superstition is further emphasized in this chapter. It is an evil omen when a girl child is born on the same day that his uncle comes for money. Then, on that very day, a flock of black crows circled his field. He took this as another sign of ill-fortune to come.

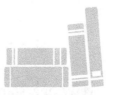

THE GOOD EARTH

CHAPTER EIGHT

. . . .

The time of evil came upon Wang Lung. No rain fell that summer, and he was forced to abandon crop after crop as it withered and died. At last the only field left was that by the Great House. Wang Lung devoted all his time to it, bringing water from the nearby moat. With the money he got by selling this meager crop, he bought another piece of land. For food for himself and his family, he had what he could save from his beans and from a little corn. O-lan took the corn cobs and ground them into powder to be eaten.

Wang Lung's uncle came looking for food. The first time he got it, but the second time Wang Lung refused him. After this the uncle went about the village telling everyone that his wealthy nephew would not give him anything to eat when he was starving. Then one night, the men of the village came and forced their way into Wang Lung's house. They stole the little food he had left, and would have stolen even the furniture if O-lan had not stopped them.

COMMENT

A picture of horrible poverty and starvation is projected in this part of the story. These Chinese peasants were totally dependent upon their land and upon the weather for survival. If the sun did not shine or the rain did not fall at the right times, the people would not have any crops. As things were, even under favorable conditions, most of them had barely enough to keep them alive from year to year. Wang Lung had been more successful than the others because of his efforts and the frugality of his wife.

The evil of their moral code is sharply defined here. The system of law and order was based on a code of honor linked to duty. Each person was bound to follow this code or be disgraced. Wang Lung's uncle was able to use this unjust code to further his own parasitism. He could blackmail Wang Lung by playing upon this duty concept. However, when the nephew, out of desperate need for his own children, refused to help the uncle, the older man turned the whole village against him. It is interesting to note that the author excuses the villagers' actions on the grounds that they were starving, and this drove them to do what they did.

The strength of the character of O-lan is again demonstrated. When the villagers want to take the very furniture from her house, she alone stands up against them. Also in this chapter the **theme** of earth is re-emphasized. Wang Lung had spent his last silver on new land. If he had kept the silver or had spent it on food, the villagers would have been able to steal these things. However, they could never steal the land from him. It was still his and would be there to be planted when the rains did finally come again.

THE GOOD EARTH

CHAPTER NINE

Now we find the family of Wang Lung reduced to absolute starvation; they have no food whatsoever. Wang Lung mixes dirt with a little water, and they eat that. It does not provide nourishment, but it keeps their stomachs from gnawing. When her time comes again, O-lan once more delivers her own child. However, as soon as it is born, she kills it rather than have it die of starvation. Wang Lung decides to go south, but he does not know how to get there since they are all so weak. Then his uncle appears with some men who want to buy his land, offering a ridiculously low price, aware that Wang Lung's family is starving. Want Lung refuses their offer and O-lan supports this decision but suggests, instead, they sell all their furnishings except the tools. The deal is made and they receive two pieces of silver.

COMMENT

This is a scene of horror: hunger and desperation can drive men to great extremes. Descriptions of the swollen bellies and the eating of dirt sharply paint the realities of starvation. But the characters cling to the one thing which they know can bring them new life - their land.

O-lan again emerges as the strong character. Whereas Wang Lung becomes angry and weak, she remains ever calm. In his mind Wang Lung compares his wife to a beast. She goes off by herself into the bedroom whenever she is ready to give birth. Moreover, she will never allow anyone near her until the child is born. She performs another animal act when she kills her own child. This may be difficult to believe of a human mother, yet there have been cases of mothers in more civilized countries killing their own children for much less serious reasons. The morality of O-lan's action, however, is not to be argued here. The action itself gives the reader an insight into the character of this strong-willed peasant woman whose fight is for survival.

The uncle is presented as the personification of evil when he deliberately takes advantage of the extreme poverty of Wang Lung. He looks well-enough fed when he comes to his nephew's house. Where he got his food the author does not say. The implication is that perhaps he might have eaten his own children. The uncle mentions that his three youngest children are gone, but does not say where. The reader is, therefore, presented with this picture of extreme horror. The author wants us to believe that these things can happen, and, in fact, there are many cases on record where they have.

THE GOOD EARTH

CHAPTER TEN

This short chapter tells of the departure of Wang Lung and his family. They had no clothes except what they wore. Each one clutched in his hand a rice bowl as a promise of the food that was to come. It took them the whole day to walk from their house through the city to the south side. When the old father weakened, Wang Lung carried him. As they passed the gates of the House of Hwang, they saw that it was locked and barred. Starving beggars lay in the gateway. At the end of their day's march, their family came near the railroad. Wang Lung had never even seen one before. He tried to decide whether they should spend their silver to ride south on it. Then, before he realized what was happening, the train arrived, and he and his family were swept aboard. They were now really on their way to the south.

COMMENT

In this chapter the author merely re-emphasizes the pitiful condition of Wang Lung and his family. Because of their weakness they needed the whole day to walk a distance of probably less than a couple of miles. The ignorance of the family is displayed by the fact that they had never even seen a railroad train although one passed so very close to their own home. Finally, there is a reiteration of the cruelty of the rich. It was said that those in the Great House still had food, yet their gates were locked, and people were left starving on the doorstep.

THE GOOD EARTH

CHAPTER ELEVEN

On the train going south, Wang Lung gave his two pieces of silver and got some coppers in return. He was able to buy some bread and a bowl of rice for his family. As the other passengers around him spoke, Wang Lung listened and learned much. Arriving in a city of the south, he went first to the market and bought six mats. From these O-lan made a hut against a long gray wall. The next day, the family went to the public kitchens where each got a bowl of rice for a penny apiece. Then O-lan and the children set out to beg. When the children made a joke of it, their mother scolded them and spanked them until they cried. In the meantime Wang Lung went out to rent a rickshaw in order to earn some money. However, he was not used to this kind of work and by the end of the day, he had only one copper penny to show for his work. Nevertheless, this plus what the family had gotten by begging was enough to pay for their rice the next morning.

COMMENT

Perhaps the most important part of this chapter is the reaction of each of the characters to his new surroundings. Wang Lung is still the proud man. He has always worked for everything that he had and would not stoop to beg. Yet, since he was a farmer, he did not know how to work in the city. The rickshaw was something new to him, and he was not very successful in this venture.

O-lan was still the resourceful one. She knew how to weave the mats into a hut. Because of the desperate need of the family she could even resort to begging. When the children made a joke of the begging, she spanked them and then used to advantage the tears they shed by displaying them to make people feel sorry for them.

The old man relied on his family's sense of duty. He was the grandfather, and so his son and grandsons would see that he was fed. The begging to him was not important. He did not concern himself with survival, but merely slept throughout the day and considered that food would come to him as his natural due.

To the children the city was completely strange; it was entirely outside their range of experience. We receive here a **foreshadowing** of what is to happen later by subtle mention of an isolated incident. The youngest son hid his money from his mother and slept all night holding it in his hand. The next morning he used it himself for his bowl of rice.

In the first chapters the rich, in the persons of the Hwang family, are shown as being cruel and selfish. However, in this chapter, a different picture is given, for when Wang Lung asks who provides the rice for the public kitchen, he is told that it is the rich. Still dubious, Wang Lung says, "Nevertheless, it is a good deed for whatever reason."

THE GOOD EARTH

CHAPTER TWELVE

....

After the first few days, Wang Lung began to get accustomed to the life of the city. However, he was still amazed by the wealth that surrounded him; he had never, for instance, seen so many different kinds of food. But he himself did not seem able to earn any extra money and whatever he had went for the morning rice. Occasionally he came in contact with some of this wealth as on the day he was hired by a woman the likes of whom he had never seen. Later he discovered that she was an American. After her ride was over, she gave him two pieces of silver, an amount double the usual fare. But this was a rare occurrence and, generally, life was excruciatingly difficult. One night when Wang Lung returned to the hut, he saw O-lan cooking some pork which his youngest son had stolen. This angered Wang Lung very much and he threw the meat upon the ground. O-lan, however, went over, picked it up, washed it, and put it back over the fire. To her, survival was foremost, but Wang Lung could not eat any of the meat because it had been stolen. Later he took the boy aside and spanked him.

COMMENT

In this chapter we get a microcosmic view of the city. Wang Lung is a stranger who does not understand much of what he sees and hears. He notices, for example, that the people speak the language in a different way than he does. Because of this, he thinks of himself as a foreigner. He hears men talk of revolution and of driving the foreigners out of China, and at first he thinks that this includes him. Later, after he sees the American woman, he realizes that he is not the foreigner.

Two things really bother Wang Lung: first, he sees that, in spite of the apparent wealth of the city, there is always a long line of people at the public kitchen. He cannot understand how there can be such abundance and such poverty side by side. Secondly, Wang Lung is disturbed by the effect which the city is having upon his family. He sees them turned into beggars. Worse yet, his youngest son has become a thief and actually seems to take pleasure in stealing. Wang Lung determines that he must go back to the land.

Again O-lan shows herself as the strong character. She encourages the children in their begging and even their stealing. This she does even though she knows that it displeases her husband. She realizes that their conventional morality will not enable them to survive this disastrous period they are struggling through.

We get at this juncture in the story the first clear indication of the time of the action. The references to revolution and to the elimination of the foreigners apparently refer to the Boxer movement in the days just before 1900. Although the time element in the story is generally vague, there seems to be little doubt that all the action thus far has taken place in the late 1890s.

THE GOOD EARTH

CHAPTER THIRTEEN

. . . .

Wang Lung and his family continued to live in the city but they were never able to get any money beyond what they needed for their daily food. During this period Wang Lung longed to be back on his land. However, this was impossible since they did not even have any seed to plant. O-lan suggested that they sell the girl child as a slave in order to get money, but Wang Lung found this too difficult to do. Although the child was a female and consequently not very worthy in their philosophy, he loved her dearly. Then one night he talked with a man who lived in one of the neighboring huts. He learned that beyond the gray wall there lived a rich family. They wore the best of clothes, and even the slave girls had jade and pearls to wear. That night Wang Lung could not sleep. He debated for hours the possibility of selling his daughter into slavery in that house. But he realized that though he might get enough money from this to return to the land, he would not have enough for seed.

COMMENT

Miss Buck draws a contrast between the very rich and the very poor. All around him Wang Lung sees shops overflowing with food, yet he himself has barely enough money to eat at the public kitchen. Each day he pulls in his rickshaw people dressed in the finest clothing, but he must wear the same clothes night and day. Then Wang Lung hears of the family that lives behind the wall with even their slaves better off than he is.

The background of the action is suggested by the neighbor man. He tells Wang Lung that "there is a way when the rich are too rich" which indicates that the time of the action is set against the political unrest of the 1890s. But Wang Lung does not know anything about politics - the only thing he wants is to get back to his land. Therefore, he does not really understand what his neighbor means and considers only the possibility of selling his daughter to a rich family where she will be well taken care of. Yet he can't bring himself to do it.

The practice of selling girls into slavery seems like a heartless one. Yet in this chapter it is O-lan who originally suggests it. She herself had been a kitchen slave in the House of Hwang and one would think that she would be the last one to suggest such a thing for her daughter. However, there are two considerations: oriental philosophy is primarily fatalistic and O-lan felt that some sacrifice had to be made before they could be allowed to return to the land. Although she would not want to do this to her daughter, she would if it were the only way. The second consideration is that for the child herself. If Wang Lung and his family remained as they were, they might all die. However, if the girl were sold into slavery, her parents would know that she would at least have food and clothing. At the same time, they would have money with which they could return home. The decision was a difficult one.

THE GOOD EARTH

CHAPTER FOURTEEN

When the spring arrived, a great unrest came over the city. Wang Lung heard men talking in the streets about what was going to happen but he did not understand, for he had spent his entire life in the country ignorant of politics. Then one day he saw soldiers seize some poor men like himself, and he was afraid. From that time on, he would not go out of the hut during the day even though he earned less money working at night. Finally, there was no work to do because all the rich people had either fled or hidden. At this point Wang Lung was more tempted than ever to sell his young daughter into slavery. However, O-lan told him to be patient. The enemy armies finally broke through the gate of the city and overran the houses of the rich. Wang Lung was swept along with the crowd into the house beyond the gray wall where he accidentally stumbled upon a rich man who begged him for mercy. Wang Lung did what he had never done before - he forced the man to give him all his gold.

COMMENT

This chapter is divided into three parts. The first part sets the mood for what is to come: the scene is of general unrest; men are speaking on street corners and handing out leaflets. Wang Lung is on the outside of this, a country bumpkin who cannot read nor understand. His only desire is to get back to his land. This is underscored by the incident of the two leaflets. One has a picture of a white man who is obviously the crucified Christ; the other is the picture of a poor Chinese who is being stabbed by a fat, wealthy man. Wang Lung understands neither one and gives the paper to O-lan to make shoe soles. Once again, the impression gained is that to these Chinese peasants political and moral questions are irrelevant next to their major concern-survival.

The second part of this chapter creates a picture of human cruelty. The soldiers go through the streets and pick men at random to carry their equipment. They place no value on human life and the population is subjected to terrorizing. Wang Lung is reduced to the level of an animal who must hide during the day and work at night. In desperation, he is more prepared than ever to sell his daughter into slavery.

The third part of this chapter describes the invasion of the rich man's house. The milling crowd swarmed through, stealing everything in sight and from each other. Wang Lung had never taken anything that did not belong to him. Nevertheless, when he came face to face with the rich man, suddenly in his desperation, he saw his chance for the necessary gold to return to his land. Notice that he does not even talk like himself: his voice is harsh and strange. This serves to demonstrate the bleakness of the peasants' existence and the horrifying lengths they must go to achieve survival.

Once more we can see the contrast between Wang Lung and O-lan. The man is the impatient one, driven by his personal desire to get back to his land. On the other hand, O-lan is patient and tells her husband to wait. Later, when the gates of the rich man's house are knocked down, she goes willingly and quickly with the multitude. Wang Lung is carried along against his will. Again it is O-lan's strength that enables her to seek this chance for survival.

THE GOOD EARTH

CHAPTER FIFTEEN

The family was able to return to the farm, using the money stolen from the rich man. Wang Lung had bought an ox along the way, and from the south he had brought good seed to be planted. At home he found his house was in shambles and his tools were gone, but the joy of being home overshadowed this latest disaster. His neighbors told him that a band of robbers had lived in his house while he was gone. Wang Lung and O-lan set about their work, and soon all was back in order. Out of sympathy and gratitude to Ching, who had once given him a handful of beans. Wang Lung gave the man some seed. He and O-lan went into town to buy new furnishings for their house and were glad to hear that the uncle had gone off to an unknown destination. Although he thought that the earth gods had been unkind, out of fear, Wang Lung went before them and lit some incense.

COMMENT

The reader should note the change in mood that occurs in this chapter since it is important to the **theme** of the story. The chapters which described life in the city were filled with a tone of anxiety, unhappiness, and unrest. In the country, all is peaceful. In spite of the famine of the year before, the land is still there ready to be ploughed again. To Wang Lung, this earth gives a sense of new hope and happiness, and survival is once again assured.

The theft of the gold - the forcible taking of someone's property - marks the beginning of a change in the personality of Wang Lung. Earlier he had thought about selling his daughter into slavery, but he could not bring himself to do it. He would not, even though starving, eat the pork which his youngest son had stolen. Now, however, in his desire for his land, he does not hesitate to use another man's gold. Even his attitude towards money changes: it is no longer a part of him and he spends it extravagantly. He does not care how much he pays for the ox so long as he gets it, and when he goes with O-lan to buy new furnishings, they get expensive ones and even buy a fancy teapot.

THE GOOD EARTH

CHAPTER SIXTEEN

. . . .

One night Wang Lung discovered that O-lan had stolen a bag of jewels from the house of the rich family in the city. In keeping with the change in him, he was pleased and wanted to buy more land. O-lan asked that she be allowed to keep two pearls from the treasure and this Wang Lung let her do. A few days later, he went into town to the House of Hwang to buy some more of their land. He was surprised by what he saw: the gates were locked and nobody was in the place except the Old Lord and a slave girl. Bandits had overrun the place and stolen everything they could take; the slaves were either driven out or carried away. The Old Mistress had died from fright. Wang Lung did not then want to buy the land because he was afraid of losing it to bandits. However, he learned from the owner of the tea shop that what the slave girl had said was true and the danger was past. And so he bought the land making sure that the Old Lord himself set his seal upon the bill of sale.

COMMENT

In the early part of the story, the author shows O-lan as a pillar of strength. His wife has been the force which has brought so much good fortune to Wang Lung. Having lived in a great house, O-lan knew just where to look for valuables and was able to steal the bagful of jewels. In this chapter, however, the reader sees the simple submission of the Chinese woman to her husband's will. O-lan meekly asks Wang Lung to allow her to keep two small pearls. This is indicative of the position of woman in oriental society; she is subject to her husband in all things.

It is made clear that the change in Wang Lung is complete. When he discovers the jewels, he does not consider whether they are rightfully his or not. As with the gold that he himself had taken, so it is with these jewels - he has them. Therefore, they are his to use for his own purposes.

The fall of the House of Hwang is another illustration of the **theme**. Wang Lung is desirous of acquiring more and more land which he can farm. The Hwangs had land, but they did not stay on it. This family which for generations had been a power, were now fallen and scattered. In Wang Lung's philosophy, this had happened because they had left the land. In order to avoid this misfortune in his family, he determines to make his own young sons begin to help in the fields. In this way, they would get the feel of the soil into their blood and bones.

THE GOOD EARTH

CHAPTER SEVENTEEN

With the fertile lands that had belonged to the House of Hwang, Wang Lung began to have great harvests. Soon he was not able to do the work himself and bought Ching's small piece of land so the man could come to work for him. As time passed, Wang Lung needed to hire more men, and so he made Ching his steward. He himself began to spend less time in the fields because he had to take the grain to market. Embarrassed by his own inability to read and write. Wang Lung determined to send his two sons to school. He began to manage his harvests so that he would always have some stored away in case of another famine. For his ever-increasing family, Wang Lung built a new house, made of earth but painted with white lime. The old house he turned over to Ching and the laborers. During these years, O-lan had a set of twins. To Wang Lung this was a sign that the heavens blessed his prosperity.

COMMENT

And so Wang Lung becomes a rich landowner. Everything seems to prosper under his direction. However, this is not merely good luck, but the result of hard work and frugality. Both Wang Lung and O-lan have put forth great effort to achieve their fortune. Wang Lung kept a careful check on Ching to test his honesty and after he was sure of the man, he made him the steward. He very properly took intelligent care of his property.

One can, nevertheless, observe, notwithstanding this great prosperity, the major changes which have taken place in the main actors - changes which have the force of destruction within them. For example, Wang Lung and O-lan had always worked side by side and shared each other's problems. Then Wang Lung stops going out to the fields altogether. He manages only the marketing and leaves the farming to Ching. Therefore, at least in a limited sense, he is leaving the thing he loves the most - his land. He also takes both his sons out of the fields. The first one he takes because he needs someone who can learn how to read and write, but he takes the second son merely to stop him from complaining about having to work. Thus, by cutting himself and his family off from the land, Wang Lung begins to sow the seeds of his own downfall.

There remain to Wang Lung two reminders of his early difficulties and of the source of his wealth. His eldest daughter, whom he almost sold into slavery, cannot speak. He affectionately refers to her as his little fool and loves her dearly because she seems to have suffered most from the results of the famine. The second reminder is the names given his two sons by the schoolmaster: Nung En and Nung Wen, meaning that their wealth came out of the earth.

THE GOOD EARTH

CHAPTER EIGHTEEN

Everything went well for Wang Lung for several years. There had been no famines, because the harvests had been good. However, one year there was a great flood and all the valleys were filled with water. Wang Lung was safe because his house was on a hill, and he still had two years' harvest stored up. But he grew impatient as there was nothing for him to do since nothing could be planted. Then he looked at O-lan, and it seemed that this was the first time that he had ever really seen her. She now appeared a very plain and simple woman. He scolded her for her appearance and complained that she never tried to make herself look more beautiful as other women did. In an angry and impatient mood, Wang Lung went to town. First he visited the old teahouse, but he decided that this was not good enough for him, and went to the new one. Here he met Cuckoo, the woman who had been with the Old Lord the day he bought the land.

COMMENT

There have been various moods projected by the concretes of the story. When the famine came, there was a time of great suffering and sadness. During the flood, however, the feeling is one of security. Wang Lung and his family did not have to worry. Others around him perished, but he had provided well for such a disaster. Nevertheless, the author does convey hints of discontent. The fact that O-lan was not beautiful had never bothered him before. In fact, on his wedding day he was very anxious that she be pleased with him. During the years that she worked by his side, he was proud of her ability. Now he looked in disgust at her big feet, her high cheekbones, and her thin hair. Before he was satisfied with her quiet ways, but now he began to think of her as a fool. No longer finding satisfaction in his own home he went to seek it in the teahouses of the town.

When Wang Lung was poor, the problem of sheer survival occupied all of his energies but he gained his strength from his ties to the land - his ability to eke out an existence from the earth filled him with self-respect. Now that he is no longer concerned with his land as such or even the way he gains his wealth, the void left by the subsequent loss of his self-respect causes him to seek something that will quiet the dissatisfaction within him.

THE GOOD EARTH

CHAPTER NINETEEN

At the teahouse there were girls whose job it was give pleasure to men who were willing to pay for it. One of these, a girl named Lotus, Wang Lung desired greatly. The beauty of this girl contrasted strongly with the plainness of O-lan. Wang Lung began to visit her every night, impatient until it was time to go to her. An astonishing change came over him, for he began to bathe daily with sweet-smelling soap and would not eat anything that had garlic in it. He bought tailor-made clothes and expensive gifts for Lotus. Finally he went to O-lan and demanded that she give him her two treasured pearls. The wife was broken hearted, but she would not disobey Wang Lung. When tears to her came eyes, she would not wipe them away, but simply began to wash her clothes more arduously than before. In this way did she let out the sorrow which she could not allow Wang Lung to see.

COMMENT

The change in Wang Lung is not a sudden one. The signs were growing more apparent as the story developed. For example, on his wedding day, Wang Lung said he hoped his wife would be beautiful. However he accepted O-lan because he was too poor to demand whatever girl he might want. Although he was a hard worker, O-lan was the one who displayed the real strength at times of crisis. On the night when the villagers broke into their house, it was O-lan who stood up to them and would not let them take the furniture. When the men came to try to buy Wang Lung's property, he could do nothing but become angry and his wife made the decision about what to sell. Later, in the city, it was O-lan who did the begging and made sure that they had food. Her strength and Wang Lung's deepening weakness were at issue in every situation.

The difficult thing for the Westerner to understand is the attitude of O-lan. Faced with her husband's unfaithfulness, she submits meekly to the situation - this woman who has had the inner resources to carry herself and her family through inconceivable horrors. Perhaps she no longer feels the deep love she once had for her husband; she can no longer respect him, at any rate. Whatever her inner state, it is apparent that she has no choice but to accept her role as woman in the conventional oriental mold.

O-lan had been groomed for this role since her beginnings. At the age of ten, she had been sold into slavery. In the House of Hwang she was merely a kitchen slave and not one of the favorites. She was forced to lose her individuality and become subject to the will of her master and later her husband. That she was able to retain enough of her identity to carry her through her troubled life is a monument to man's ability to survive no matter what pain he may have to endure.

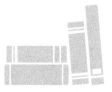

THE GOOD EARTH

CHAPTER TWENTY

Wang Lung had not seen his uncle since the time of the famine. But the man appeared one day with his wife and son. Nothing could be said when the three of them made themselves at home because it would be a dishonor for a man to turn away his relatives. The uncle's wife was very shrewd, and she realized right away that Wang Lung had fallen in love with another woman. She gave him the idea to buy Lotus and bring her to live with him and promised to help him arrange things. He had his laborers build a new apartment for Lotus. O-lan was, of course, very sorrowful, but although Wang Lung was moved by this sorrow, he refused to give in to it. Instead he continued with the preparations, and when Lotus arrived, she found that the rooms prepared for her were very beautiful. But there also was something that Wang Lung had not bargained for. Lotus insisted that the woman Cuckoo come with her as her maid.

COMMENT

In this section the concept of evil is reiterated. First the uncle comes with his family to live with Wang Lung, taking advantage of the Chinese code of honor. He knows that his nephew cannot refuse him hospitality without being disgraced. Then the uncle's wife, for her own purposes agrees to help Wang Lung bring the girl Lotus to his house. Thirdly, there are Lotus and Cuckoo who are willing to sell themselves to Wang Lung for silver, clothing, and a good place to live. Lastly, of course, there is Wang Lung himself. He knows that he is being unjust to O-lan. He is even moved by her expressions of sorrow. Nevertheless, he will not yield to her. He is so filled with his own lust and his own frantic desires that he is willing to do more for a girl whom he barely knows than he ever did for the woman who has shared and saved his life. O-lan has borne his sons, but now she is too old and ugly for him. Thus, he casts her aside for the young and beautiful Lotus.

THE GOOD EARTH

CHAPTER TWENTY-ONE

Before Wang Lung took Lotus into his home, he had not foreseen the difficulties that would arise. O-lan, however, took out her displeasure not on Lotus, but on Cuckoo. She was angry to see this woman in her house, for she remembered how Cuckoo had treated her in the House of Hwang. Then, too, Cuckoo took advantage of Wang Lung: when she went to the market, she always bought very expensive food. The third difficulty arose when the old father discovered Lotus in the house and was furious with his son for bringing a harlot into his home. Then one day the twins brought the poor fool daughter into the court of Lotus. Wang Lung was angry when he heard Lotus refer to his beloved daughter as an idiot. Eventually, all of these things caused Wang Lung's love for Lotus to cool. He no longer saw her as the sweet young thing whom he visited at the teahouse. Therefore, when he awoke one morning to find that the waters had receded, he was glad for the opportunity to go out to the fields to work.

COMMENT

In this chapter, the reader learns that fundamentally Wang Lung is not an evil man. It is true that he does an evil thing in bringing Lotus into the house but he learns to regret it. Wang Lung constantly tries to justify himself by saying that he does only that which others have done. Yet, Underneath the surface, Wang Lung is ashamed. He cannot talk to O-lan because he knows that has been unjust to her. By the same token, he loves his children, especially the poor fool who has suffered so much. When Lotus curses them, he is very angry at her.

In this chapter the author also shows us another side of the character of O-lan. In the early part of the novel, this woman has always appeared as a strong character. But in this instance even her strength cannot bear up under the injustice. She sweeps openly. More than this, however, is the resentment that she shows toward Cuckoo. The woman had made life unbearable for O-lan when both were slaves in the House of Hwang. Now O-lan tries to make life as miserable as possible for the other woman. Unfortunately, it is Cuckoo who gains from this treatment. In order to make things more pleasant for her, Wang Lung has a stove constructed in the apartment of Lotus. He also allows Cuckoo to do her own shopping so she can buy whatever luxurious food she desires. Therefore, O-lan's treatment of Cuckoo avails her of nothing.

However, the desire for the land is not dead in Wang Lung. When the waters recede, he goes out to the fields. In this way, we are reminded of the **theme** of the novel. Wang Lung is soothed by the feel of the good earth beneath his feet.

THE GOOD EARTH

CHAPTER TWENTY-TWO

With the coming of the good weather, Wang Lung was back in the fields. Again he was the farmer instead of the idle rich man that he had been during the time of the flood. His harvest was good that year, and he kept it until the prices were high. In the market he was very proud of his eldest son who did his figuring for him. On the way home one day, Wang Lung determined that it was time that he got a wife for this son. However, he wanted a beautiful one for him, and one who came from a great house. Many months passed and none was found. The boy began to grow moody. He would not eat and would skip school. During the day he would spend time in the town. When he would hear about this, Wang Lung would become angry and beat the boy. O-lan, however, understood what was the matter. One day she went in to her husband to speak with him. O-lan told Wang Lung that the boy was like the young lords she had seen in the House of Hwang. He had nothing to do, and, therefore he was melancholy. Wang Lung then decided that he must soon find a wife for his son.

COMMENT

In this chapter the cycle of life is beginning to take its full swing. Wang Lung's eldest son is ready for marriage. This presents an interesting situation for the reader who is curious about Chinese custom. The boy is only about seventeen years old at this time. He was twelve when he started school, and only a few years have passed since then. However, the only comment made about age is that by Wang Lung who says that they can marry him early. From this, of course, the reader can conclude that the average Chinese boy did not marry quite so young. However, it is the reason for the marriage that is interesting. The boy has nothing to do and is restless because of this. His father won't encourage him to work in the fields to keep him busy. What he plans to do instead is to marry him off, and in this way try to give some responsibility.

It is interesting to note O-lan's solution to her son's restlessness. She wants her husband to buy a slave for the boy. This seems like strange talk to come from a woman like O-lan who had been a slave and had hated her existence. She also hated having the slave Cuckoo in her house. However, both of these are extremely personal things for O-lan. First of all, she had been only a kitchen slave, and therefore badly treated. Secondly, O-lan disliked Cuckoo personally and not because she was a slave. However, the real reason O-lan wants a slave for her son seems to be to keep him out of trouble with his father. If the boy is kept busy with a slave girl, he will not have time to annoy Wang Lung

There is a good contrast drawn in this chapter. When Wang Lung was young, he was too busy working to think of anything else. If he left his work, he would not have food to eat. On the other hand, the son does not have to work. If he never does anything, there will still be food for him in his father's house.

Another point that the reader should note is the action of the younger son. He tells Wang Lung that his brother was not in school. This is in keeping with what we know of this boy's attitude so far in the novel. Also it will help the reader to understand some of the things that occur later.

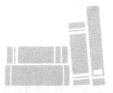

THE GOOD EARTH

CHAPTER TWENTY-THREE

. . . .

After his talk with O-lan, Wang Lung went into the court of Lotus. This girl told him that the grain merchant, Liu, had a daughter whom the eldest son might marry. However, Wang Lung was still hesitant. Then one morning the son came home drunk. Wang Lung was especially angry after he discovered that his uncle's boy had taken the eldest son into town. He decided that it would be better for the son to be married immediately. But this could not be arranged because Liu thought his daughter was still too young for marriage. In his anger, Wang Lung wanted to send his uncle's family away. The uncle showed him the signs of the robber band to which he belonged, and Wang Lung knew he was trapped. If he sent his uncle away, the bandits would overrun his land and lay waste to it. Then that summer the locusts came, and Wang Lung's attention was taken up with fighting them. By building fires and moats, he was able to kill many locusts and save some of his fields.

COMMENT

In this chapter Wang Lung seems overburdened with difficulties. He has his eldest son to worry about, and he has his uncle whom he must now fear. Then the locusts attack his fields. Of all these problems, the only one that Wang Lung can fight is that of the locust. The problems of nature he knows how to fight, but not the problems of humans. The reason for this seems to lie within Wang Lung himself. He had been a poor farmer, but he was a good worker and knew how to save his money. Also he knew that land was the thing of greatest value to the farmer. Therefore, he bought more and more of it. Gradually he became rich. With his increased wealth, he thought that he should live and act in a particular way. He wanted to be like the Old Lord in the House of Hwang. However, he was too simple and uneducated. He forgot that it was the land that had made him wealthy, and so he left it to tend to the marketing. He even took his sons away from it. In other words, in imitating the Old Lord, he did exactly those things which had brought about the downfall of the House of Hwang.

One of Wang Lung's problems is apparently insoluble. That is his difficulty with his uncle. This man had always given him trouble. However, Wang Lung had accepted it because he did not want to be disgraced by driving his relatives out of his own house. Now Wang Lung learns that his uncle is a member of a band of robbers. He realizes that this is the reason why his lands have never been overrun. Those robber bands were one of the great problems in China. They were large and powerful, and no one ever did much to rid the country of them. They could come and go as they pleased. If Wang Lung sent his uncle away, they would undoubtedly attack his lands. As long as he allowed his uncle to stay with him, he would be safe. Therefore, he had no choice but to endure the problems that his uncle's family created for him.

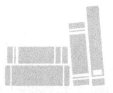

THE GOOD EARTH

CHAPTER TWENTY-FOUR

One day after Wang Lung had come back from the fields, his eldest son came in to him. The boy wanted to go south to study for he had learned all he could in their town. However, his father was angry and would not let him go. Lotus then tried to influence Wang Lung on the boy's behalf but she did not succeed. Finally one night O-lan came in to her husband and told him that the eldest son was spending too much time in the court of Lotus. Wang Lung refused to believe this, and so O-lan left him. However, the next day he pretended to go to look at a distant field, went only a short way, and came back by a different route. Going to the court of Lotus, he discovered that his son was indeed there. Angered, he made a whip and beat both his son and the girl. Lotus swore that she had done nothing but speak with the boy. But Wang Lung did not know what to believe. Therefore, he decided to send the boy south and to let him stay there.

COMMENT

We again see the impotence of Wang Lung. He is in reality an ignorant man who does not know how to cope with any human problem. For example, he cannot see the obvious illness of O-lan. She has become thin and gaunt in appearance. A bulge in her stomach indicates a probable tumor. But Wang Lung is unconcerned and never thinks of telling her to hire a servant to help her with the work.

However, Wang Lung's greatest offense in this chapter is against his son. Whatever the boy is, Wang Lung is in great part responsible for it. He thought that he could direct the boy's life in all things. First he wanted him to work in the fields. Then he decided that the boy was too good for this and so he sent him to school. When the boy became restless with nothing to do, Wang Lung determined that he would have him married. He wanted his son to follow his every whim. But the boy had a mind of his own and was not satisfied with his life the way it was. Therefore he wanted to leave home and be on his own for a time. The unfortunate fact was that Wang Lung could not understand this desire. As a result, he had to send his son away in anger rather than with love.

THE GOOD EARTH

CHAPTER TWENTY-FIVE

After the eldest son had left, Wang Lung decided that he would provide for his other children before they became too restless. Therefore, he made arrangements for the second son to be apprenticed to the merchant Liu, the father of the eldest son's betrothed. While he was with Liu, he also arranged a betrothal for the youngest daughter who was almost ten. When he told his daughter of his plans for her, she commented that Wang Lung did not love the mother of his children. He was bothered by this, and so he began to take more notice of O-lan. Finally he realized how sick she was, and he made her go to bed. But it was too late. The doctor had little hope of her living. Wang Lung had gone through much trouble to arrange everything for his family. But this one thing he could do nothing about. Now that it was too late, he realized how much O-lan had meant to him.

Comment

In this chapter Wang Lung behaves like the shrewd businessman that he was. He goes to the house of Liu to talk of the apprenticeship; if Liu had come to his home, Wang Lung would have had to give him food and drink. Wang Lung feels that if his second son is working in the grain market, the boy will be able to tip the scales in his favor. Wang Lung further solidifies his connection with the merchant Liu by betrothing his youngest daughter to Liu's son. In this way, Wang Lung feels that his family is completely provided for. The oldest son is a scholar; the second is a merchant; and the third he will make a farmer.

The words of O-lan which the little girl repeats probably sum up the character of Wang Lung better than any others could. "You are too kind and weak for pain," the girl says. Thus she explains many of the actions of O-lan. For example, the wife would not allow her husband into the bedroom until after each child had been born. Later, in the city, she did the painful begging and allowed Wang Lung to go through the city looking for work. The reader can also see the truth of the little girl's words in the actions of Wang Lung himself. When everything went well, he was happy. However, whenever anything went against him, he became angry and often wept.

In contrast to the character of Wang Lung, that of O-lan is virtually the opposite. She never complained of her pain unless she were asked about it. In spite of everything, she continued her daily work and never asked for help. Even on her sickbed, she does not want Wang Lung to spend money for her recovery. She feels unworthy of this, very probably because of the way in which Wang Lung had treated her. The love of O-lan for her husband is certainly a great and a strange one. It is evident that she centered her existence around him.

THE GOOD EARTH

CHAPTER TWENTY-SIX

. . . .

O-lan did not die immediately, but lived on for several months. During this time, Wang Lung spent each night in the bedroom with her. He would try to comfort her, but he could not rouse any great tender feeling for her. On the other hand, he could not go near Lotus either. Cuckoo and the children tried to keep the house in order, but they could not do this very well. During these days while O-lan lay sick, she would mumble words about her past life and Wang Lung learned many things about O-lan which he had never known before. One day O-lan asked that her new daughter-in-law be brought to the house so she might see her. Then O-lan asked that the wedding be performed before she died. Wang Lung sent for his eldest son so that he might be married. After this took place, O-lan died. Then, a short time later, the old man died. There was much sorrow in the house of Wang Lung.

COMMENT

The story of O-lan's death might perhaps be called the story of her life. Throughout the long months of her illness, she would murmur phrases from her youth. Wang Lung learned, for example, of the beatings that his wife had suffered. This explained why she had stood between him and the eldest son when Wang Lung would whip the boy. He heard his wife cry out in a heartbreaking voice for her mother and father and was able to understand O-lan's unwillingness to sell their own daughter into slavery. Then O-lan had a moment of justice. She sent for Cuckoo. When the slave arrived, O-lan told her that she was still a slave in spite of her manipulations, while O-lan had become the mistress of her own house.

This death scene is a pathetic one particularly so because of Wang Lung. He had used his wife to help satisfy his desire for land and for sons. However, he had never appreciated her. He looked at her ugly face, and not her beautiful spirit.

The scene with Cuckoo explains why O-lan had always been so silent even in the face of great difficulty. Her youth had been filled with so much suffering that O-lan was satisfied just to know that she had risen above slavery and had had children. What's more, even though Wang Lung did not return her love, O-lan's children did. Her eldest son came home to be married so that his mother might see this event take place before she died.

Wang Lung, however, has not really changed. When he goes for a coffin, he buys two because he will get one third off the price. Also, although he is moved by the suffering of O-lan, he cannot arouse any tenderness for her. He is still the shallow man that he always had been.

The reader learns of another strange Chinese custom in this chapter. After O-lan dies, she is not buried immediately. Wang Lung goes to a geomancer to find out the best time for burial. The geomancer, by studying lines and various geometric figures such as the triangle, is supposed to be able to foretell good and evil. Since Wang Lung wanted his wife to be buried at a good time, he followed the geomancer's advice and waited three months before he had the funeral for O-lan.

THE GOOD EARTH

CHAPTER TWENTY-SEVEN

. . . .

Soon after the funeral of O-lan, Ching came to Wang Lung to tell him that there would probably be another flood that year.

Wang Lung became very angry and cursed the gods who had so little concern for men. When the floods came they were worse than they had been the last time. Many people died, and many houses were washed away. However, Wang Lung really had no worries since he had a great store of food on hand. The one thing that really bothered him was his uncle's family. One day the elder son came to complain because the uncle was getting better food than anyone else and Wang Lung told his son the truth. This made the son angrier, and he suggested that they get the uncle's family to use opium which would eventually make them harmless. Wang Lung, however, did not at first want to do this. Then one night, the uncle's son attacked Wang Lung's youngest daughter. The father was angry and took his daughter to the house of Liu for safety. On the way home he bought some opium to give to his uncle's family.

COMMENT

Once more the reader gets a good view of the character of Wang Lung. His riches have given him a certain type of courage. He is not afraid to curse the gods, but they are not there in person to take out their wrath on him. On the other hand, Wang Lung's riches have also made him fearful. He grants his uncle's every wish lest the band of robbers overrun his lands, and he locked his gates against the villagers through fear that they might come and rob his stores of food and silver.

The eldest son of Wang Lung was very much like his mother in appearance and character. For years Wang Lung had been taking care of his uncle; first he did this through respect, and then through fear. However, the eldest son became angry when he saw the uncle's family being treated better than anyone else. When he hears the story of the band of robbers, he plots how he can murder the uncle's family. But when Wang Lung could not bring himself to murder a man, his son hatched another plan. They could buy opium for the uncle's family, and keep feeding it to them. After a while they would be so addicted to it that they would be completely harmless. Both of these plans sound very much like something O-lan might suggest. It is similar, for example, to her treatment of Cuckoo: she tried to starve this woman by keeping her away from the water cauldron so that she could not cook her food.

Wang Lung's love for his children again shows itself in this chapter. He is afraid to do anything to his uncle's family until the night that the uncle's son attacks his youngest daughter. This makes Wang Lung very angry. He humbles himself to ask Liu, the merchant, to take the daughter into his house for her own protection. As an excuse, he tells Liu that the girl's mother is dead and there is no one to protect her virginity. Then, on the way home, he buys six ounces of opium. He gives into this plan only as a defense for his children; he will do anything to protect them from harm.

THE GOOD EARTH

CHAPTER TWENTY-EIGHT

....

Wang Lung gave his uncle the opium. The uncle and his wife became addicted, and both of them started to waste away because of it. The uncle's son, however, continued to be a nuisance. Wang Lung's eldest son was very angry that nothing was done about his cousin. He suggested to his father that they move into the great house where the family of Hwang had resided and leave the uncle's family in the country house. Wang Lung was not moved by the complaints of the son about his nephew, but the thought of living in the great house appealed to him. He went to town to ask the second son's advice. He also believed it a good idea for the family to move into town. When Wang Lung went to see about renting the house, he remembered how he had been ashamed the first time he had gone there. Going into the courts, he saw the dais on which the Old Mistress had sat. On an impulse he got up on it: then and there he decided to move into the house.

COMMENT

This might be regarded as the chapter of development because in it we see many of the characters undergoing subtle changes. Wang Lung, of course, has not changed much. He is still proud of his wealth and shrewd in the way he uses it. He sells the grain at a high price and lends out money at interest. However, he now does something which he would never have done before. He tricks his uncle into using the opium, although he knows that it will destroy the old man. He stoops to this level to defeat an enemy whom he would not drive out openly. Also the false pride of Wang Lung is given full play in this chapter. He buys slaves to show that he is an important man and agrees to move into town. Under no circumstances would he have moved into town in his younger days.

The character of the eldest son is fully revealed in this chapter. The reader sees him as so sophisticated that nobody would ever suspect that his father had been a farmer. This son wants nothing to do with the land. All he wants is to live in town as an aristocrat and a scholar supported by his father, thereby enjoying all the luxuries of life and none of the responsibilities.

We also see the second son fully grown and developed. We remember him as the son who stole the pork. He was also the one who refused to stay on the land while the eldest son was in school. These characteristics are now fully developed. This son has grown into a shrewd merchant, and in many respects he is just like his father. For a wife he wants a woman who can do a good job of overseeing the household work and has not come from too rich a home. In other words, he wants a wife who will work hard and ask little in return.

The third son, the twin, is also mentioned in this chapter. The father has planned that he stay on the land. However, he does not seem content to do so. When he goes about the farm with his father, he keeps his head down. The reader gets the impression that he, like the eldest son, is dissatisfied with the way his father has planned his life.

THE GOOD EARTH

CHAPTER TWENTY-NINE

. . . .

Wang Lung sent his eldest son to make arrangements for renting the House of Hwang. This done, the son and his wife, Lotus and Cuckoo and the slaves moved into town. Wang Lung himself was not yet ready to leave the land, so he remained in the country. Then he sent Ching to get a wife for the second son. This was soon done, and the marriage arrangements were made. There was more good news for Wang Lung when his uncle's son decided to join an army in the north. Then the eldest son's wife gave birth to her first child, and there was great feasting and rejoicing. Amid all this joy, however, there was the sad news of Ching's death. Wang Lung eventually decided to move into town. He took his third son and his mentally incompetent daughter with him. Wang Lung no longer wanted to work his lands, but he would not sell them. Therefore, he rented them all out to the village farmers who were anxious to use the good lands that he had.

COMMENT

In this chapter the cycle is almost completed. Ching, Wang Lung's last link with the soil, has died. None of his three sons was content to stay in the country. Even the youngest one - he whom the father had picked to be the farmer - did not want to stay on the land. Wang Lung himself is too old for the work, but he will not sell that which he values most highly. Therefore, he rents the land, shrewdly arranging for half the crops as his fee. When the wife of the eldest son gives birth to her first child, Wang Lung thinks once more of O-lan. His wife had delivered her own children without complaint, and had then returned to the fields to work. She would bring the babes with her and nurse them herself. With the son's wife it is different: she must have her slaves about her when she gives birth and her cries of pain can be heard throughout the entire house. Then, after the child is born, she wants to hire a servant to nurse it for her.

We are introduced here to the Chinese practice of ancestor worship. Now that Wang Lung is the head of a great and rich household, his sons convince him to set up tablets to be worshipped on the feast days. The names of ancestors were inscribed on these tablets. As each man died, his name would also be inscribed. Then the family would burn incense in front of the tablets as a sign of respect.

The superstition of these Chinese people is again shown by various incidents. For example, the wife of the eldest son has taken a dislike to the poor fool daughter. She does not want this other girl near her. She says that to look upon the poor fool would be to mar the infant with which she is pregnant.

THE GOOD EARTH

CHAPTER THIRTY

Wang Lung thought there was nothing left for him to do but sit and enjoy himself. This was not true. The eldest son was discontent and would continually come to his father for money to buy new things or to fix another part of the house. After Wang Lung had given this son a great deal of silver, the second son came and complained about how much was spent on useless articles. Then Wang Lung sent for his youngest son because he had heard that this one did not want to be a farmer, and finally gave him permission to have a tutor. It seemed to Wang Lung that the only happiness he had was with his grandchildren. Within a space of five years, he had seven-four boys and three girls. Each of these had his own slave to care for him. In this way the household was greatly increased in number. During this time, the old Uncle died, and Wang Lung buried him on the hill near his father and O-lan. Then, out of pity for the old woman, he brought his uncle's wife to the house in town. Giving her a room in the outer court, he instructed Cuckoo to get a slave to tend to her.

COMMENT

The family of Wang Lung was now established in the town. He was the head of a great landed family, and people referred to him as Wang the Big Man or Wang the Rich Man. This greatly pleased him, for he cared very much about what people thought of him. From his very early days. Wang Lung had this desire to be pleasing in the eyes of other men. In the House of Hwang, on his wedding day, he was ashamed of his appearance even before the gatekeeper. During the years that followed, he kept his uncle's family because he did not want to be disgraced for turning out his relatives. Now the eldest son uses this trait in his father to get from him whatever he wants. He continually tells Wang Lung that the family will lose the respect of the people if they do not have this or that luxury. So greedy is the young man that he uses an underhanded means to get the poor people out of the frontcourts. He offers the son of Hwang more money in rent than these people can afford to pay. Therefore, they must move out. Wang Lung's family now have the entire house for themselves; they have replaced the House of Hwang completely. In fact, so complete is this takeover that the poor people now direct their hatred and jealousy against Wang Lung. They speak of him with the same words that the poor in the huts of the city had spoken of the rich: "Someday, when the rich are too rich, something will happen. The poor will come back."

In his own way the second son was as greedy as his brother. Whereas the eldest could not get enough money to spend, the second could not get enough to save. Thus does the author show the reader two forms of greed. The one leads a person to want all sorts of luxurious things without any desire to earn these things. On the other hand, the greed of the second son was a love of silver for its own sake; he never spends any money unless he has to. Even at his own wedding he divided the guests according to their position in life and fed each group that food it was accustomed to.

If the author does emphasize any good point in this chapter, it is the Chinese love of family. In his old age, Wang Lung found his greatest pleasure while playing among his grandchildren. Through them he saw himself and his name being carried on down through the ages.

THE GOOD EARTH

CHAPTER THIRTY-ONE

Wang Lung had heard rumors of war all during his lifetime. Nevertheless, the only experience with it had been the winter he spent in the South. His second son told him that the armies were getting close to them. Then an army came sweeping out of the northwest. Among the soldiers was the son of the old uncle. When he saw Wang Lung, he realized that here was a place they could all stay and told the men with him to enter the courts of the House of Hwang. Wang Lung was disturbed by this, but he could do nothing against the army. The soldiers turned the outer courts into a shambles, and still Wang Lung dared not complain: he feared the son of the uncle just as he had feared the uncle himself. To appease him, Wang Lung offered him a slave girl for his pleasure. Even this created a problem, for the man chose a girl who was afraid to go with him. However, Wang Lung sent another girl in her place, and the man was satisfied. After about a month and a half, the soldiers departed.

COMMENT

The cunning of the second son is well demonstrated in this chapter. He wants to hold his father's grain until the armies come closer so he can charge higher prices. Later, however, when the armies actually do come to the town, he is the first one to be frightened. He tells his father not to anger the soldiers, but to let them do whatever they want.

The first son also shows his true nature. Although he hated his cousin, he had always been afraid of him. He had wanted to kill him secretly, and then he had plotted the use of the opium. Now he stands quietly by while the cousin insults his wife. It is true that the other man is armed, but the eldest son says nothing in the defense of his wife. This seems to be real weakness rather than momentary fear. He could have uttered some word of praise for his wife, such as "She has borne me good sons." After all, this man was his cousin and would not be inclined to anger at a remark like that. Also, as a Chinese, he would very probably have appreciated this type of Chinese praise for a woman. Nevertheless, the eldest son remained silent in the face of this ridicule of his wife.

Throughout this chapter, Wang Lung is typically himself. He hates this son of his uncle and having the army camped in his house. However, he does not show the great fear that his two sons do; he resorts to cunning. When the cousin goes in to see his mother, she is, of course, in a very poor state because of the opium. But Wang Lung cleverly turns the blame upon her. He convinces his cousin that the mother demanded the opium, and because of her age, he let her have it.

The kindness of Wang Lung shows itself again in the incident of Pear Blossom, the slave girl whom the uncle's son desired.

When Wang Lung saw the fright of the young girl, he could not bear to send her to the other man. Therefore, he dared to cross his cousin by sending a different slave to him. Fortunately, the man was satisfied.

A short incident in this chapter, foreshadows some events to come. During the scene which describes the decision about whether or not to send Pear Blossom to the uncle's son, the author describes the characters as standing silently about. But she mentions the youngest son specifically, standing there with his hands clenched and his brows drawn down over his eyes. Apparently he has a very special interest in this girl.

THE GOOD EARTH

CHAPTER THIRTY-TWO

. . . .

After the soldiers left, Wang Lung and his sons determined to restore the house to the condition it had in been previously; it took a year before everything was complete. Then Wang Lung thought that he could have some peace, but again he was wrong. The wives of the two sons began to fight which, of course, led to bitterness between the brothers. The eldest was already jealous because the second son was the father's steward. This hatred between the wives made the situation worse. Wang Lung also had a problem with his youngest son. This boy had been very much ignored by his father. However, while the soldiers were camped in the outer courts, he had listened to their adventurous tales and decided to become a soldier. The father was distressed and tried to coax his son to do some other thing. However, no matter what Wang Lung promised him, the boy would not change his mind. He had heard many tales of the changes to come in China, and he wanted to be part of them.

COMMENT

When Wang Lung was poor, he had no problem except that of having enough to eat. Now he has all kinds of problems, many of which are the result of the irrational handling of his riches. The jealousy between the two sons, and the hatred between their wives are both the result of this mismanagement. The eldest son wants to spend the money, and the second son wants to save it. If they earned their silver, they would be too busy to concern themselves with such pettiness.

Wang Lung has other problems too. In her old age, Lotus has become very jealous. She no longer has her beauty to protect her. Therefore, when she sees Wang Lung paying attention to the young slave, Pear Blossom, she is annoyed. Wang Lung himself cannot understand why he should be so attracted to this young girl. He is jealous when he sees that his youngest son likes her also. This feeling, however, is not too difficult to explain. Wang Lung saw his essentially empty life fading away from him, and tried to recapture the dreams and energies of his youth through the young girl.

The most interesting part of this chapter, however, is the scene with the younger son. This boy, who had started his studies late, had become an eager student. He read everything that was available to him. He begged his tutor for books about the old China. While the soldiers were living in the outer courts, he listened to their tales. Therefore, he had a very good idea about everything that was happening in the country. He was filled with the stories of the revolution and of the changes that were to come; he wanted to be part of them. But when he told his father, Wang Lung did not understand for he was old and filled with the old ideas. When the youngest son told him that the land would be free, he did not understand what this meant. To Wang Lung the land was free because it belonged to him, and he could use it as he wished. The son, however, was speaking of Socialism. Land would no longer be owned by individuals; the state would take their property declaring private ownership a political crime. The young boy called this new policy "freedom" because he accepted the promises of the new order that the land would be distributed "free" to all.

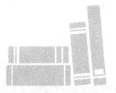

THE GOOD EARTH

CHAPTER THIRTY-THREE

Wang Lung could not stop thinking about Pear Blossom. Finally, one night he took her into his court with him. Although she was but a child by comparison with him, he felt that he must have her by his side. For a time he was able to keep this affair a secret. However, Cuckoo saw the girl slipping out of Wang Lung's court and threatened to tell the family. The old man was concerned about this, but he allowed Cuckoo to tell Lotus and to offer her gifts so that she would not be angry. Then each son in his turn came to see for himself what was taking place. The father had not feared either of the older sons, but he was afraid of the youngest one. The boy was very angry, and said that he would now go off and join the army. After he left, Wang Lung fully realized what he had done. He had taken for his own the maid whom his youngest son had wanted. The next morning, this son was gone, and no one knew where.

COMMENT

This chapter might be called the "Folly of Old Age." However, the observant reader will realize that it was not mere foolishness that led Wang Lung to do what he did. A large part of the reason was loneliness. His family had paid little attention to him since they had moved into the great house. So long as they could have the money that they wanted, they did not care about the old man. Even Lotus in her shallow way had made Wang Lung feel unwanted.

This chapter might also be called "Realization" because in it Wang Lung finally understands many things which were unclear to him before. For example, he realizes that he is an old man and that he should not do those things which young men do. He should not have taken Pear Blossom for his own. Then too, when the second son comes in, Wang Lung realizes that he is no longer interested in the harvests or the droughts. He had spent his whole life working and worrying about these things and considered that now that he was old, his sons should care for him as he had cared for his old father.

Wang Lung had always concerned himself about what his eldest son thought. He was afraid to hurt this one's pride. But this was not to be the case anymore, for now Wang Lung saw this son for what he was - a man big in body but afraid of his own wife; a man who was concerned only with appearing nobly born. This son had been born of the land, but he was a weakling. His old father was a stronger man than he was and knew it.

There is an element of **irony** in the coming of the third son to see his father. This boy had been the most ignored by Wang Lung. The father really had very little knowledge of what this son was like. He had destined him for the land without even asking the boy what he wanted to do. However, this is the son who goes off to the revolution. He is the one who will do the most to destroy the old ways that Wang Lung liked so well. The sad part is that this might have been avoided if the father had paid some attention to this son. Instead, he even took for himself the very girl whom his son wanted. By doing this he killed the last ray of hope that the boy would stay with him.

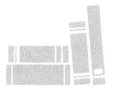

THE GOOD EARTH

CHAPTER THIRTY-FOUR

Wang Lung's desire for Pear Blossom soon died. He was fond of her and kept her in his court because she wanted to stay. When he realized that he might soon die, Wang Lung asked Pear Blossom to poison the poor fool daughter. Instead, she promised to take care of the other girl after her father died. Then Wang Lung told his sons to prepare his coffin so that he would be able to see it before he died. In this way, he could die in peace. As time passed, Wang Lung began to go out to the country. He could not work the lands, but he enjoyed being there. He would sleep against the old wall as his father had done. One day he overheard his sons talking about which lands they would sell. Very disturbed, he insisted that they should never sell any of them. The sons told Wang Lung that he had misunderstood them; they would never sell his lands. The old man was content when he heard this. However, the sons were insincere; they knew that they would sell the land as soon as their father had died.

COMMENT

With this chapter the cycle is complete. Wang Lung had started as a poor young man with a small piece of land. By thriftiness and hard work, he had built himself into a wealthy landowner. No matter what the temptation, he had never sold any of his lands. Now he is about to die and with him the land also will go. The sons want no part of it; they merely want the silver that it will bring.

Wang Lung's love for his demented daughter is still strong. He knows that there will be no one to care for her when he dies. He has bought some poison, but he cannot bring himself to give it to her. He asks Pear Blossom to do this deed for him, However, she promises to take care of the other girl. In this incident, we have another example of the Chinese attitude towards human life. O-lan had once killed her own new-born child rather than see it starve. Now Wang Lung wants to poison his daughter rather than see her suffer from lack of care.

The reader will recall that in the earlier chapters Wang Lung accepted the fact that his life was merely his turn to work the earth. Others had gone before, and others would come after him. Death was not something he feared. When Wang Lung sees his coffin, it is a reminder to him that he will die but he is resigned to the thought. He knows that he will receive a good burial and be put back into the earth with his ancestors where he can rest peacefully.

THE GOOD EARTH

. . . .

WANG LUNG

The principal character in this novel. The entire story revolves around his life. Perhaps it is more accurate to say that the story is of his life. The novel begins with Wang Lung as a young man and ends with him as an old man near death. It tells of his rise from a poor man to a rich landowner.

Wang Lung is a peasant, but not a simple man. He is obsessed with the idea of land; to him this is the only real wealth. It is the only thing that cannot be stolen from a man and so every time he has an extra silver he buys another piece of land. Even when he is starving, he will not sell his security. Instead he goes to the south to try to earn money for seed so that he can return to his land and plant new crops.

If Wang Lung has any great fault, it is his desire to be pleasing in the sight of other men. As a young man, he is self-conscious about his appearance. He is shy even before the gatekeeper at the House of Hwang. Later, he takes care of his uncle because he does not want to be disgraced. He is careful about the feelings of everyone and gives them whatever they want so that they will be satisfied. The only exception to this seems to be O-lan, his wife. At the beginning of the story, he wants her to be pleased with him. Nevertheless, he gradually develops to a point where he does not seem to care about her. For example, he marries a second wife, and he takes from O-lan two pearls which she loves.

There seems to be no explanation for Wang Lung's treatment of O-lan. The author gives a feeble one when she explains that Wang Lung sees no beauty in her. But as mentioned before, Wang Lung, having lost his self-respect, feels great dissatisfaction for his life and the people who were part of his unhappy existence, and this is far more to the point. It is probable that he saw O-lan as a threat to his masculinity as she was so clearly the stronger of the two. It is also true that the marriage was arranged; he did not choose O-lan. However, their many years together and the close sharing of fundamental values should have developed some authentic affection for her.

Although he is shrewd in his business dealings, Wang Lung is not a strong character. He works hard on his land, but he does not know how to deal with people. The laborers who work for him appear to be the only ones who are afraid of him. Even O-lan, until Lotus comes, is able to do things that displease Wang Lung. For example, she won't let him throw away the stolen pork. The second son is allowed to go to school simply because he keeps complaining. Lotus, and even the slave Cuckoo, get whatever food and gifts they want from him. Therefore, the family of Wang Lung seems destined to fall, not because they lose respect for the land, but because Wang Lung fails to assert himself as the strong head. He does not represent a strong authority, and he does not teach his family to love those things which he values.

O-LAN

The second most important character in the story. Although she dies before some of the important action takes place, her influence is felt throughout the entire novel. As opposed to Wang Lung, she is a strong person. Very probably her husband would not have become rich or even survived if it had not been for her. During the months that the family spent in the south, it was O-lan who kept them together and alive. Her begging provided most of the money for their food and her strong will and determination prevented Wang Lung from selling his daughter into slavery.

In order to understand O-lan, the reader must always bear in mind that as a child she had been sold into slavery by her own parents. Because she was not a pretty girl, she was made a kitchen slave. This meant that she was among the lowest of the slaves and did the worst jobs. Therefore, O-lan developed a great ambition. Someday, after she had been given in marriage, she would return in triumph to the great house. This she did when she brought her first-born son to see the Old Mistress.

O-lan has all the qualities that a good Chinese wife should have. She is an extremely competent housekeeper. She is thrifty and never wastes anything. Very seldom does she ever ask anything for herself. When the first child is born, she asks for silver to buy cloth for some new clothes. Then, after the family returns from the south, she asks to keep two small pearls. Otherwise she does not ask for anything, not even a servant to help her with her work when she is ill.

The mystery of the character of O-lan is her silence when Wang Lung brings Lotus home as his second wife. She was greatly hurt by this, but she said very little to her husband about it. This was not because she was afraid, since O-lan had never been afraid of anything or anyone, including her husband. For example, when Wang Lung would beat the eldest son for missing school, she would intercede and receive the blows intended for the boy. The only explanation, therefore, of O-lan's attitude in the matter of Lotus is that she has the oriental resignation to fate. Although she is deeply hurt by Wang Lung's attitude and actions, she knows that she is subject to him. As her husband, he is her master under the law. In spite of all she has contributed towards making the family successful, O-lan, as a woman, has no legal claim to anything. Therefore, her only alternative is to live in the household as the mistress and mother of the family, but not as a wife to Wang Lung. Her position would be similar to a divorced woman in America who is hired as a housekeeper and maid for her ex-husband and his new wife. Only O-lan's position is worse: she has no choice in the matter but to remain.

THE OLD FATHER

He plays very little part in the action of the story. Nevertheless, he is important to the mood of the novel as he represents the old China. He sits against the wall and sleeps in the sun while the young people work to take care of him. Even during the famine, when the family moves south, he does nothing. Wang Lung, in his starved condition, must carry the old man upon his back. When the rest of the family begs or steals or works, he merely sleeps. The only life shown by him is when he eats or when he laughs because a new son is born. The only activity he shows is the loud demonstration he makes when he sees Lotus in the household.

The reader might interpret the presence of the Old Father in the story as a sign of the Chinese respect for old people. However, if we consider the underlying **theme** of the novel showing China as a changing country, we can give a symbolic interpretation to this character. He is the old China which has done nothing to improve itself. In his old age he is still poor and backward. In times of trouble he is a burden to the young; they must carry his extra weight. Wang Lung, who must move forward in order to survive, has to bear the extra burden of his father. In the same manner, the new China has to bear the burden of the old, backward China. Another aspect of this concept is the fact that the only real disturbance that the old man causes is when he wakes up and finds Lotus. In other words, the old China does not like change. When it sees anything new, it gets up to complain loudly. However, like the old man, it is too tired to do anything. Therefore, it goes back to sleep, and lets the world change. Slowly it dies.

THE ELDEST SON

As do the others, he represents a part of the **theme**. Although he comes from a poor and hard-working family, he wants to be a scholar and an aristocrat. He really does not care where the money comes from just so long as he does not have to work for it. In this way he is like the old Chinese lords who bled the people for money to satisfy their own shallow desires for pleasure.

This son is a weakling. When his father beats him, he says nothing. He wants to go to the south, but he will not go on his own. He waits until the father sends him away. Later on he stands silently by while his wife is insulted. He is, therefore, a symbol of the old Chinese aristocracy which crumbled so easily in the face of the revolution.

THE SECOND SON

Also representative of the **theme**. He is the shrewd old China which took advantage of the needs of the people. He holds the grain until the prices are high. He does not want to spend money unless he has to. But he too is a weakling. When the army comes from the northwest, he is the first to let them have whatever they want. He never speaks unless it is to get something for himself, as when he wanted to go to school, or to tell his father how to save more money. His kind also fell because of their cruelty to the people and their insensibilities.

THE YOUNGEST SON

The symbol of the new China. Wang Lung has ignored this son to such an extent that he has no understanding of him. The father simply decided that this son would stay on the land and considered it no further. However, the youngest son had ideas of his own. He wanted to learn and to improve himself. After he learned about his country, he wanted to do something for it. This son is not afraid to act. When his father takes the maid whom he wanted for himself, he runs off and joins the army. The last that is heard of him is that he is some sort of official in the new Chinese government.

THE POOR FOOL

Her father's favorite because she reminded him of the suffering that the family had endured. She does nothing but play with a little piece of cloth. Very literally she does not even know enough to come in out of the rain. She must always have someone to look after her. Therefore, she symbolizes what hunger and suffering can do to a people. If China is a weak nation at the time that the action of the story takes place, it is because famine and oppression had reduced the peasants to virtual serfs. Even Wang Lung had thought of selling this girl into slavery in order to help himself get back to his lands. Fortunately, he did not do so, because the girl would undoubtedly have been killed by whoever bought her; a fool would be good for nothing.

THE SECOND DAUGHTER

Not too important to the plot, she has no characteristics to speak of. As a girl she is given in marriage to another family. She and the poor fool provide a contrast with the sons. Wang Lung thinks that perhaps daughters are better because they provide very little burden for their family. Sons must be provided for, but daughters can be given in marriage to other families. Therefore, their own parents need not worry about supporting them during their lives.

THE OLD UNCLE

An antagonist in the story presenting a conflict for Wang Lung. As a lazy and selfish man, he imposes himself upon the nephew. Wang Lung can do nothing to rid himself of his uncle. Until his death, this character is a constant threat taking every possible advantage of another's weakness. However, his greed contains the seed of his own destruction. He seizes upon the opium which eventually kills him.

THE UNCLE'S WIFE

Like her husband, is an evil person. She takes advantage of every situation which she can manipulate. When Wang Lung brings Lotus to his house, the uncle's wife makes friends with her. In this way she can share the good food which Cuckoo prepares for Lotus. However, her greed, like that of her husband, is the cause of her downfall. She too falls victim to the opium habit.

THE UNCLE'S SON

Also is a lazy and vicious man. Whereas the uncle is mainly interested in food and shelter, his son is interested in all types of animalistic pleasures. For example, he takes the eldest son to the teahouses of the town. Later he tries to attack the second daughter. When he goes to join the army, it is for excitement, but he says that he will not stay around when there is fighting. Like his an animal cowardice while theirs is more of an intellectual sort. He survives by his emotions. They plot and connive for what they want.

LOTUS AND CUCKOO

They can be considered together since they are fundamentally the same type. Each is a shallow person who tries to get whatever she can for herself. However, their motivation is not the same as that of the uncle's family. These are two women who have never been married; they are on their own. In the China of those times, this was almost an impossible situation. There was really very little that they could do but what they did. There was no way for them to present themselves to good families for marriage. Custom was against them. By the same token there was little work that they could do. A woman on her own in China had very little chance for survival. Therefore, Lotus and Cuckoo were forced by necessity to sell themselves.

CHING

A lesser character in the story, but he represents the old Chinese man who is no more than a slave to his land. When the land fails, Ching must starve. He showed his kindness when he gave Wang Lung a handful of beans for O-lan. later Wang Lung rewarded him by making him the steward of the lands. In this job Ching was honest and successful. When he dies, Wang Lung loses his last connection with the land. In a sense, the death of the superstitious old Ching signified the end of an era.

THE OLD LORD AND THE OLD MISTRESS

Important in the story only because they are the ones whom Wang Lung envies. As a young man, Wang Lung looks to these people as examples of what he wants to become. By the end of the novel he has established himself as the head of a great family.

THE GOOD EARTH

CONTROVERSIAL NATURE

From the critical viewpoint, *The Good Earth* and its author have been controversial. There are some who think that her work is great and others who consider her a hack. In our study of her life, we mentioned the dispute about the subject of this novel. Some Chinese intellectuals objected to the fact that the hero was a peasant rather than an aristocrat. Miss Buck's answer to this was that she was writing about the people she knew best: the common people of China.

AWARDS

Her defenders point to the fact that this novel was a best seller for two years, and that in 1932 it was awarded the Pulitzer Prize. However, this does not necessarily make it a great novel. We do not wish to take away from the value of this prize, but it is, after all, an annual award. When it is given to a novel, what is meant is that this novel was the best one written during a particular year.

The award does not of itself mark the work as a great American classic. Only time and the reading public can perform this feat.

In order to prove her ability as a writer, Miss Buck's supporters also point to the fact that she won the Nobel Prize for Literature. However, this prize is not generally given for any particular work. It is given rather as a reward for a contribution toward world peace and human understanding. Consequently, when Pearl Buck received this prize, it was because of the subject of her works rather than for their literary value. She had written with understanding about the problems of the Chinese people and had tried to arouse sympathy for these problems. Besides, she had written the biographies of her parents, showing how they had worked to help the Chinese improve themselves. Therefore, she justly received the award, but not necessarily because she was a great writer.

CHARACTERIZATION

In *The Literature of the American People*, George Whicher has this to say about *The Good Earth*:

"Here for almost the first time Oriental characters were treated by a western novelist as more than picturesque accessories."

These words refer to Miss Buck's use of a Chinese setting and topic, and to her using Chinese as her main characters. In many American novels, the Chinese simply fill the roles of servants or insignificant characters. In this work, the author makes them her chief subject. Nor are they simply foreigners or curiosities: they are presented with universal characterizations. Wang Lung, for example, has the same problems that men everywhere have: the problems of the married man who must care for his family. He has to struggle against poverty and against injustice. The solutions which Wang Lung finds are not necessarily the same that someone else might find, but they are believable, human solutions. He is the Twentieth Century type of anti-hero found in the novels of authors like Sinclair Lewis. In other words, although he has risen from poverty to a position of wealth, he is not a happy, satisfied man. He contains within himself the seeds of his own self-destruction.

DEMOCRACY

The Literary History of the United States says that Pearl Buck established a link between the United States and China, indicating a brotherhood of Democracy. The statement is made in reference to all the works of Miss Buck, but it can be applied in particular to *The Good Earth*. The novel tells the story of the changes that took place in China during the first quarter of the twentieth century. It does this by relating the story of a family. Through its evolution, we see some of these changes. As a nation ruled by a small clique of aristocrats, China was decaying. Various other groups tried to save their country. Unfortunately, they were not successful, and now the Communists have control.

In this respect, probably one of the best things that Pearl Buck accomplished in *The Good Earth* was to give the world a picture of the condition of Chinese women. Through the characters of O-lan and Lotus, the author shows the hardships that Chinese women had to endure. By so doing, she brought these problems before the English speaking audience. She hoped in this way to arouse interest in them, and somehow to cure this evil of woman servitude in China.

EPIC NOVEL

In *Cavalcade of the American Novel*, Edward Wagenknecht includes his discussion of Pearl Buck's work in the appendix. By doing this he classifies her as a minor novelist, although he does not say this in so many words. However, if he considered her as a novelist of importance, he would have included his study of her in the main body of his work alongside Hawthorne, Twain, and Lewis. Therefore, his discussion of her works is short and to the point. He says that *The Good Earth* is more **epic** than dramatic. By this he means that this novel is merely a long story which relates a series of events about a hero. In this case the hero is Wang Lung, and the series of events is his life. The events are related to each other in an orderly fashion, and they come to a rather nice, orderly conclusion. However, there is no high point, or **climax**, in the story. The actions do not build up to any turning point where a momentous decision by Wang Lung will bring about a great change in his life. Also, there is no dramatic interplay among the characters in the story. Wang Lung cannot be called a **protagonist** because he has no great conflict to solve. There is no antagonist in the novel; no one who causes the hero any great significant problem.

In an **epic**, therefore, there is no purposeful progression of events; each chapter is an isolated incident. Wang Lung is the hero throughout the novel; and as each difficulty arises, he takes care of it. But the lack of dramatic impact is due to the fact that there is no great moral conflict to resolve.

Neither the drought, nor the flood, nor the dispute with the old uncle is the central issue in the book. Rather, the purpose of the book is to project a **theme** telling the story of Wang Lung's life.

Pearl Buck has said that she is greatly indebted to the Chinese novel whose purpose is entertainment. By these words, she strengthens the argument against her own work: her avowed purpose is to entertain people by telling them a story. This is not in the classic tradition of literature in the western world.

While entertainment is an important purpose of literature, education-showing the reader lessons in good and evil, whether moral or social-has consistently been considered the principal purpose of literature by its most serious students. Therefore Pearl Buck's simple style - her attempts to reach the masses by telling them a simple story - has been greatly criticized by this group.

The best feature of *The Good Earth*, therefore, would seem to be its characterization. The author has created people who happen to be of a particular race, but who are universally identifiable. Her clear style makes the work easily understandable. Her story of simple, everyday people makes it interesting.

THE GOOD EARTH

Question: Explain the Chinese custom of marriage.

Answer: The Chinese custom of marriage is centered around the premise that the woman is inferior to the man. Her position in life is to be the servant of the man and the mother of his children. She has no say whatsoever in the selection of her husband. Although the marriages were arranged by the parents, a son could tell his father what type of girl he wanted. However, neither boy nor girl met until their wedding day. All the arrangements were made by their elders for them. When the girl came to the home of her husband, she usually brought a dowry. This was generally some articles of clothing and household goods. If the family were rich, then some money would also be included. There was no wedding ceremony performed. The mere fact that one family gave a bride and the other accepted her meant that the wedding had taken place. However, sometimes children would be promised in marriage while they were still young. This simply meant that they could not be promised to anyone else. The marriage itself took place when the girl moved in with her man.

Question: Why is Wang Lung the main character in the novel?

Answer: Wang Lung is the main character in the novel because it is the story of his life. The novel begins when he is a young man and ends when he is near death. All the action of the novel revolves around him. The main reason Wang Lung is presented as the principal character is because he symbolizes the **theme**. He is the one who tries to cling to the old ways by making the acquisition and not the earning of wealth his primary concern. He instilled this disregard for real values into his family. Therefore, when the old China falls, it is Wang Lung's shallow ideas that will fall with it.

Question: Why is O-lan the most admirable character in the novel?

Answer: O-lan is the most admirable character in the novel because she is a person of great courage and fortitude. Throughout her entire life, O-lan is faithful to her most fundamental value-survival. It is apparent that none of them could have survived without her inner resources. She works side by side with her husband and bears him good sons. When his strength falters, she is there to help him. For example, when the three men come to try to buy their land cheaply, O-lan is the one who makes the decision to sell only the furniture. Later, Wang Lung turns against her for no apparent reason other than her lack of beauty. However, although she knows she cannot prevent his actions, she still maintains her dignity. All of her life she manages to retain some vestige of her personal identity-borne out by her courage in the face of unspeakable horrors - while struggling to conform to the oriental mold in which she was cast.

Question: Explain the Chinese peasant farmer's dependence upon the elements of nature.

Answer: The Chinese peasant farmer had no source of wealth except what he could get from his land. There were no large industrial cities for him to go in search of work. If his land did not produce food for him, he would starve. This explains Wang Lung's desire to have as much land as he could. However, the earth does not of itself produce crops; rain and sunshine must come at the right time and in the necessary amounts. Too much of either could destroy the crops. This is what happened in *The Good Earth*. In the early part of the novel, there was a drought which meant that the farmers could not water their crops. They had no irrigation systems for bringing water from lakes and rivers. Later on in the novel, there were two great floods. Again the farmers could do nothing. Since there was no other place for them to get food, they starved, and many died.

Question: Why does Wang Lung take care of his uncle's family?

Answer: There are two reasons why Wang Lung takes care of his uncle's family. The first is the Chinese duty-morality centered around the family. This included not only one's sons and daughters but all relatives. Anyone who would not take care of members of his own family would be disgraced. Of course, the uncle could have taken care of his own family if he were not so lazy. However, he took advantage of this Chinese custom in order to get Wang Lung to provide for him.

The second reason why Wang Lung took care of his uncle's family was his fear of the robber bands. These outlaws had no respect for anyone. They plundered and killed wherever and whenever they liked. If they had thought that Wang Lung were wealthy, they would have overrun his lands. Since the uncle was apparently a member of these bands, Wang Lung's land was safe as long as he kept his relative there.

Question: Explain the period of time presented in the novel.

Answer: The time element of *The Good Earth* is somewhat vague. We know that it is in the modern era. Because the book was published in 1931, we know, of course, that it concludes before that time. When it begins is difficult to determine. The author mentions that Wang Lung is about seventy-five years old. However, we do not know his age at the beginning of the story, although he might have been about thirty. We know that he was in the southern city around the time of the Boxers. This would pinpoint the date 1900. Also, in the last chapter, the author speaks of the revolution as having taken place. In this way, we can conclude that the main action of the story is probably between the years 1890 and 1927. It is impossible to be more accurate than that.

Question: What does the Old Father represent in the novel?

Answer: The Old Father represents the old China. He is a man tied to the tradition that the young must take care of the old. Also, like the old China he is asleep while everything around him is wide awake. The whole world is changing, but China remains the same. By the same token, the old man is deaf. He cannot hear anything. The old China is also deaf. She cannot hear the noises that are going on around her. The old man sleeps against the wall. In the ancient times, the Great Wall protected China from her enemies. The old man awakes only to protest the coming of Lotus. The old China protested the coming of new improvements. Lastly, the old man dies a peaceful death. The old China died too, but her death was violent.

Question: What are the major turning points in the life of Wang Lung?

Answer: There are three instances in the life of Wang Lung which may be considered as turning points. The first, of course, is his marriage to O-lan. It changes Wang Lung's way of life from that of a single man to that of the married one. Also it introduces the influence of O-lan on the action of the plot. The remainder of the novel develops from this event.

The second, and probably the most important, turning point in the life of Wang Lung is when he takes the gold from the rich man. Before this time, he is very careful about doing only what is right and honorable. For example, he refuses to eat the stolen pork, and he spanks his son for having stolen it. However, in this scene Wang Lung is desperate. He will do anything to get back to the land. When he demands gold from the rich man, Wang Lung does not even recognize his own voice. From this point on, however, he does many things that he would not do before. For example, when he discovers that O-lan has the bag of stolen jewels, he does not worry about where they came from. He just uses them. His driving ambition is to store up wealth so that he will never have to leave the land again.

The third crucial point in the life of Wang Lung is the incident concerning Pear Blossom. He takes this girl for himself. When his sons come to see him about this, he finds that he no longer cares what they think. Before, this he, was very concerned about his sons. Now he is afraid only of the youngest, but he doesn't understand why. After this event, the story easily comes to its conclusion. The cycle of Wang Lung's life is over.

Question: Why is *The Good Earth* a story of people rather than a story of events?

Answer: Some novels emphasize the events. The action of the story is more important than the people who perform these actions. However, this is not the case with *The Good Earth*. In this novel it is the people with whom the author is concerned.

It is true that the setting is in China and that the characters are Chinese. However, except for some incidentals, the story could be moved to some other locale. Wang Lung, for example, could be an American farmer who works his way up to a position of prominence. He has the ambition and the ability to do this. Also, his treatment of his family is not necessarily Chinese. Many American fathers try to plan the lives of their children. Others spoil their children by giving them whatever they want. American men have also been known to desert faithful wives. The fact that O-lan is Chinese, therefore, does not mean that she is the only wife that has ever been mistreated. Likewise, what we have said about Wang Lung and O-lan could be said for most of the other characters. Even Ching, the old Chinese peasant, could be instead a poor American sharecropper. Therefore, we see that the abstract characterizations of Miss Buck's people are more important than the actualities of their world.

Question: What are some of the strengths and weaknesses of *The Good Earth*?

Answer: As a story, *The Good Earth* is clear and to the point. The author does not wander away from her **theme**, nor does she moralize. There are no subplots that distract the reader from the action of the main plot. Also the characters are real, and, for the most part, believable. The reader can easily picture them as existing.

One great weakness of the novel is the author's sense of time. By this we do not mean that she does not refer to particular dates so that the events of the story can be placed historically. Actually, doing this would weaken the story. What we mean is that the author loses her sense of chronology. For example, the youngest daughter is not quite ten when she is betrothed. Then, apparently, many years pass during which much happens.

Nevertheless, she is not quite thirteen when she is attacked by the uncle's son. Then, again many years apparently pass during which much more happens. But, when the youngest son - this girl's twin, and therefore the same age-appears before the father, he is still a young boy. This kind of error is the most blatant weakness in the book.

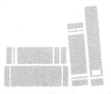

THE GOOD EARTH

Pearl Buck's style in *The Good Earth* has been compared to old Chinese novels. Actually, it is a simple, direct narrative style. There are no complicated techniques such as cut-back or stream of consciousness. The narrative moves along smoothly towards its conclusion. By the same token there are no complicated subplots or subthemes. Wang Lung is the central character; the actions of all the other characters relate directly to him. No one in the story performs any action which is independent of the main action.

Perhaps the greatest strength of the style of Pearl Buck in *The Good Earth* is the manner in which her characters perform. No matter what any one of them does, it is always in keeping with his personality. Nevertheless, none of them can be described as stereotypes; their motivations are too complex. In O-lan, the reader sees a person who is fundamentally good. Yet she does some seemingly wicked things. She steals the jewels from the rich man's house. Worse than this, she kills her own child. But both of these actions are consistent with her character and the context of the situations she is involved in.

THE GOOD EARTH

. . . .

The **theme** of this novel is not a complicated one. The author is trying to show how a family can rise from poverty to a position of wealth. However, the rise in itself is not the crucial element; the background against which this rise takes place is more important. Wang Lung lives in an era of change. China has been a backward country in many respects. Her principal fault, however, was the existence of two distinct classes of people - the rich and the poor. The rich led a pseudo-cultural existence unconcerned with the realities of the country. The poor in between fighting plagues, floods and famines, were taxed as well. On the fringe of these two groups were the robbers bands who plundered wherever they could.

The old aristocracy of China was rotting away as the result of its own greed. Waiting for their chance was a group of young intellectuals who claimed that they were going to bring about many reforms. However, since the time that *The Good Earth* was written in 1931, history has shown that these revolutionaries only intended to replace the old aristocracy with a new one. They had little intention of doing anything constructive for the poor people. As a result, when the Communists came after World War II, they were able to take over China very easily.

Where does Wang Lung fit into this picture? He is a poor man who knows nothing besides the value of land. Therefore, he spends his entire life building up a large estate. However, he builds according to the old system. As he becomes richer, he separates himself from his own people and he allows himself and his family to fall into the same faults that the other rich had. Then he allows his sons to separate themselves from the land - that which had given them their wealth. Although the author does not carry the story through, the reader knows that this family is destined to fall.

The earth-theme is predominant throughout. As a man pours his energies into his land he reaps great benefits - survival and self-respect. Miss Buck appears to be saying that the only thing that can truly save China is the honest toil of her people who must be allowed to claim the rewards of their efforts without oppression.

BIBLIOGRAPHY

· ·

FICTION

In listing these works, we will simply give the title and the date of publication.

The Good Earth, 1931 *Sons*, 1932 *A House Divided*, 1935 *Dragon Seed*, 1942 *The Promise*, 1943 *Kinfolk*, 1949 *Letter from Peking*, 1957

NON-FICTION

Of Men and Women, 1941 *American Unity and Asia*, 1942 *What America Means to Me*, 1943 *China in Black and White*, 1945 *Yu Lan, Flying Boy of China*, 1945

BIOGRAPHY

The Exile, 1936 *Fighting Angel*, 1936 *My Several Worlds*, 1954

ABOUT THE AUTHOR

George F. Whicher, "The Twentieth Century," in *Literature of the American People*, ed. By Arthur Hobson Quinn, New York: 1951.

Spiller, Thorp, Johnson, and Canby, *The Literary History of the United States*, New York: 1953.

Edward Wagenknecht, *Cavalcade of the American Novel*, New York: 1952.

Printed in the USA
CPSIA information can be obtained
at www.ICGtesting.com
LVHW051600280724
786727LV00008B/457

9 781645 423706